"Dr. Foster has written a very informative book on how family and entrepreneurship God's way! As someone who has been in my own home-based business for 14 years and home schooled for five years at the same time, I sincerely hope that her book helps more people find their own path to making work and family mutually supportive."

—Bonnie St. John, author of *How Strong Women Pray* and webTV show host at www.bonniestjohn.com

"Bellandra Foster has overcome obstacles in her personal and professional life with quiet strength and implacable grace. Her new book is a practical and spiritual guide to getting things done and managing success. It offers a clear-eyed road map to a balanced life—and a rock steady source of inspiration and hope."

—Jeff Gerritt, Editorial Writer and Columnist Detroit Free Press

"Dr. Bellandra B. Foster has carefully penned her debut book, *For Love and Money: Seven Guidelines for Achieving Success in Your Home and Business,* and it is timely and will surely help us to prioritize family and business. This wonderful work is systematically divided into seven simple and attainable principles, with God as the primary focus. For example, Dr. Foster acknowledges that seven is God's perfect number in the book's introduction. Further, Principle One is *Have a Conversation with God,* instructing us to maintain priorities in pursuit of our entrepreneurial dreams. Scripturally supported throughout, Dr. Foster's principles, formulas, and pointers, when applied, help us to achieve our business goals while successfully balancing our personal and family responsibilities. A recommended read!"

—Kevin Wayne Johnson, Give God the Glory! book series www.writingforthelord.com

"As an author, entrepreneur, wife, and mother, I found *For Love and Money* to be an excellent guide on how to do it all! The Biblical references on how to recognize your passion, purpose and vision were right on target, as were the simple family suggestions, such as 'cuddle time'. Dr. Foster's book is a must-read for fledgling and seasoned entrepreneurs."

—Tiffany L Warren, playwright and national bestselling author of *What a Sista Should Do* and *Farther than I Meant to Go, Longer than I Meant to Stay* www.tiffanylwarren.com

"The foundation of our great society is our families. However, all too often we allow our pursuit of success/money to get in the way. Dr. Foster says, "A lot of Dads have been replaced by child support checks, and moms have been replaced by fast-food restaurants and the babysitter." It is OK to seek fortune, but don't forget about God and your family.

Dr. Foster captures the essence of the delicate balance between God, family and money in her new book entitled *For Love and Money: Seven Guidelines for Achieving Success in Your Home and Business*. Read it and follow her principles/guidelines and you will increase your chances of success.

Remember what Booker T. Washington said, "Success is to be measured not so much by the position that one has reached in life as by the obstacles which he has overcome."

—Larry C. Harris, MD and author of *It All Starts at Home:*
15 Ways to Put Family First (Revell)
www.itallstartsathome.com

"A God-guided whirlwind! That's a word I used to describe Dr. Bellandra Foster. In her book, *For Love and Money,* she gives other women tips and proven strategies to help them find balance and success in being a wife and mother while making the money! A must read for any woman who understands that she is called to be a God-guided whirlwind and entrepreneur!"

—Dr. Gail Hayes, Success Strategist and author of *Daughters of the King:*
Finding Victory Through Your God-Given Personal Style
www.daughtersoftheking.org

"Dr. Foster helps you move beyond your fears and comfort zone to realize your dream as an entrepreneur. She equips you with the tools to achieve success and balance through your spirit life, both for your business and your home."

—Stephanie M. Clark, author of *Life As A Single Mom: It Isn't Easy, Or Is It?*
www.mydaughterskeeper.org

FOR
LOVE
AND
MONEY

FOR
LOVE
AND
MONEY

SEVEN GUIDELINES FOR ACHIEVING
SUCCESS IN YOUR HOME AND BUSINESS

DR. BELLANDRA B. FOSTER

Pleasant Word
A Division of WINEPRESS PUBLISHING

Pleasant Word (a division of WinePress Publishing, PO Box 428, Enumclaw, WA 98022) functions only as book publisher. As such, the ultimate design, content, editorial accuracy, and views expressed or implied in this work are those of the author.

ISBN 13: 978-1-4141-1034-9
ISBN 10: 1-4141-1034-0
Library of Congress Catalog Card Number: 2007904179

DEDICATION

To my sons, Lance Michael Foster and William Aaron Foster. May you always be blessed by the anointing of the Kingdom of God. I thank God for allowing me to be your Mom—I Love You!

CONTENTS

ACKNOWLEDGMENTS

To my Lord and Savior, Jesus Christ. *I love you!* You placed me on this planet with a specific purpose in mind. You blessed me with the desire to please You in all I do.

I am thankful for loving and supportive family and friends. I thank you for my parents, George and Ella Benefield, who have transitioned to their place with You in heaven. I thank my parents for raising me with continuous love, discipline, and reverence of You, Lord. Throughout my life, You have always shown yourself to be faithful as I walked within the comfort and love that your Word provides.

You have continued to guide me throughout my life by blessing me with my husband, Michael. When I prayed for a husband who would love me for a lifetime, you answered my prayer. I honor my husband for taking on this role in my life, and we thank you for predestining our marriage. I am thankful for our sons, Lance Michael and William Aaron. I love them more than words can express, and I am truly blessed by them. Thank you, Lord, for your guidance and reassurance in fulfilling my ultimate and highest calling of being a wife and mother.

I am thankful for the staff of BBF Engineering Services, P.C. I truly appreciate the effort, dedication, and loyalty of the entire staff. Your guidance in prioritizing the most significant things in life has served to be invaluable. I thank you for showing me how to deal with the circumstances that arise when life is just not fair.

Thank you, Lord, for your blessings, for love, and for saving my life and my soul.

INTRODUCTION

Seven is God's perfect number. The number representing progress, perfection, and divine completion. Biblical scripture tells us God rested on the seventh day, after creating heaven and earth. There are seven primary planets in astronomy. Even dice games recognize *seven* as a lucky roll.

Now what if I told you I could offer seven guidelines to becoming your own boss? That's it—seven. Seven basic principles you can follow to begin a successful business that can grow and prosper in more ways than you ever imagined. Would you believe it? Or would you think it was impossible? Now, let's throw something extra into that mix: What if I told you there was a way for you to combine raising your family while building a business at the same time?

"Not without a stunt double," you say? Well, I'm here to let you know that you can have the best of both worlds—because I do, and I've never been a stuntwoman! You can have peace in your home, happy children, and a husband or wife who loves and supports you. You can also be the president and CEO of a business you feed with care and nurture in the same ways you feed and nurture your beloved family. As hard as this might be to believe, there's an opportunity just waiting for you. Read on and take my advice. You'll wonder why you waited so long to do what you thought was impossible.

It's not easy to get out of the frame of mind that we have to be on somebody else's payroll. After all, that's the way of the world, right? There are many times more *employees* than there are employers. The competition to be a job-holder is greater than the competition to be a business owner. Our parents and their parents, for as long as most of us can remember, went to work for companies that employed hundreds or thousands of other people. We remember them getting up early, coming home late, and being glad to receive overtime pay. They might even explain to us that the new bike or dance lessons we wanted depended on whether their boss gave them any extra hours for the week. They came home tired, sometimes sore, and sometimes complaining. But they were glad to be able to provide for us, and we were thankful for the rewards that came from having caregivers who could hold a job.

Not much has changed since that time, especially the fact that most adults still seek stable employment with established businesses. But the political power of major companies and corporations is more and more apparent these days. Big businesses have long been a main attraction for cities that want to increase their economies and make their communities appealing. Who wants to move any place where they can't find a job and support their loved ones? This is why so many mayors meet with company executives. It's also why there are tax breaks and incentives offered to businesses as ways to encourage them to base their headquarters and new offices in communities that need them. All communities need jobs.

What has changed, on the other hand, is not for the better. There are far more struggling families, single-parent homes, and couples who can't even work together—let alone live together—to raise their children. It's not just the men and women who are affected anymore. Failed relationships and poor decisions seem to be creating strain in our children's lives, now more than ever before. A lot of dads have been replaced by child support checks, and moms have been replaced by fast-food restaurants and babysitters. Although it's true that there are a lot of social problems contributing to these issues, another important root cause is simple lack of parental direction.

One result of a lack of parental direction is a legacy of family members who lead "ragged" lives. A ragged life produces many negative circumstances, such as: failed marriages, wayward children, substance abuse, poverty, unaccomplished goals, unhealthy bodies, and other evidences of a life in disarray. How does any adult successfully take on the responsibilities of a job and family when he or she may still have other personal goals and desires? Nobody wants to feel like life is over when it should be just starting. But unfortunately, the choice seems pretty clear for men and women today—commit to supporting a family *or* pursue career goals and dreams. With the outlook that only one can be done, but not the other, it's not so surprising that couples end up unhappy in their marriages and that others practically turn their backs on loved ones in order to chase after their dreams.

By now you may be thinking to yourself, *I'd love to pursue my career goals and raise my family, but I don't see any mayors offering tax breaks to help me open my business.* So, how can this information be helpful to you? First you have to recognize that all the focus on big businesses leaves more room in the market for entrepreneurs. There is considerably greater excitement about new products and services when they are offered in communities saturated with corporate presence.

Think about the last time you visited a bakery or florist. These types of businesses often are independently owned and almost automatically generate customers who don't feel like they can get the same care or quality at large companies. But regardless of the area that interests you, consider the chance for your new enterprise becoming successful, compared with the limited amount of jobs you could seek at someone else's company. The next step is to simply decide you're ready to go for it. The big challenge is to pursue the goal without sacrificing the strength and stability of your home.

Making a choice was *never* a choice for me. Being a happily married mother of two was fulfilling in my private life, but I had driving professional desires also. My educational and professional goals could know no boundaries. I had come too far from my humble beginnings as a young girl from a family in Flint, Michigan, to let anything stand between success and me. No matter where you are in your life, this is an important perspective: You've come too far *not* to succeed. Do you believe that? Think about it.

The drive to work hard for your purposeful goals is the first step. It doesn't mean you have to come from the same family background I did. Or that you have to be a certain age, have a certain education, or hold a list of special achievements. Believing you've come too far requires only that you recognize you've got something to offer and that there is a purpose for your existence. My purpose and desires included being a loving wife and mother, but God also placed the desire and ability within me to own my company and assist entrepreneurs in professional business pursuits.

There is no more natural and healthy sense of obligation than the duty to care for your family and yourself, but caring for yourself means more than just caring for your body. It means expressing the gifts and talents God gave you. So, whatever your personal or professional experience, why not act on it? You've heard stories of people who started developing their gifts and talents into great careers when they were down and out. What if Jackie Joyner Kersee decided she couldn't compete in track and field because she suffered from asthma? She would never have won Olympic medals. What if Samuel L. Jackson talked himself out of a stellar acting profession because he'd had many adverse life challenges come against him as a young African American male. He would not have become one of the most sought-after actors in Hollywood.

If these obstacles didn't stop two of the world's best-known entertainment and sports figures, being devoted to a family shouldn't stop you. Your family is a blessing. By pursuing your career goals as an entrepreneur, you can be a blessing to them. Don't look at it as a gamble, because in everything there are risks involved. People have worked for twenty years and been laid off without warning. Factories, offices, and even hospitals have shut their doors, leaving employees on their own to start looking for work and find new ways to support themselves and their households. So, no career choice can truly guarantee security for us. But, in the seven guidelines that will be discussed here, you will gain an understanding of things, such as timing, administration, and self-promotion, which will help ensure you make the smartest and most effective moves toward starting and developing a business. You will also learn ways to create a healthy balance between your home experience and your experience being your own boss.

So where do you start? In anything related to business, research is a most valuable tool. You should always start with a broad vision, even if you already know exactly what kind of enterprise you'd like to pursue. That's a good thing. When you know the desires of your heart and have a clear vision of what your company or organization will do, it helps you to put your plans in motion. The main purpose of research, however, is to help assess the strength of your plan. When you don't have such a clear idea for your business, research serves an even greater purpose. Research can help you identify the specific area of need that your idea—*your company*—will help fill.

For example, suppose you've always been interested in fashion. You've loved fine clothes for as long as you can remember. But you realize that nobody (except a model) gets paid to dress up and wear fine clothes. And here you are, short to average height, not looking like you've missed a meal in a while. You don't want to be on the runway or in magazines, anyway. You just know that working in fashion would satisfy you ten times better than your job as a receptionist.

Researching the field at your local library or on the Internet will give you a sense of the industry. There may be trends in the business that you'd not heard about, but that you'll need to know in order to identify the path you should take. Maybe you thought you could never make it in fashion because you'd have to uproot your family and move to New York, but through research you learn there's some new move toward cyber-modeling that lets you work at your PC. Findings, of course, will vary, depending on the industry you explore and the degree of investigation you do. Remember, there's no such thing as too much preparation, and research is what gets us prepared. Here's some general information and recent, year 2003 data from Bizstats.com that may help you begin investigating the field where your business opportunity is waiting:

- More than 25 million businesses filed income tax returns in America in year 2000.
- Of the 25 million business entities that file annually, there were 17.6 million sole proprietorships, including 670,000 real estate agents, 600,000 childcare workers, and nearly 1.8 million construction, special trade contractors.

- Limited Liability Companies (LLCs), businesses that function in a flexible structure between sole proprietorship, partnership, and corporation status, have been the preferred identity of most new businesses.
- There were nearly 18 million sole proprietorships—businesses owned by one person—in the year 2000.

Of the millions of businesses that filed income tax returns, only twenty percent reported having employee payrolls. What no statistics can show is whether these business owners spent quality time supporting loved ones. Did they show up for dance recitals and baseball games? Did they cook meals and help with homework? Did they make their husbands and wives feel appreciated?

We'll probably never know if they did these things, because we don't know all of these people. But, by following seven guidelines, *you* can do all of these things without sacrificing your personal or business goals. You can truly have it all, and I will tell you how...

HAVE A CONVERSATION WITH GOD

Did you ever hear the story about the man God instructs to push the rock in the roadway? It's many times the man's size, a very large boulder that's much heavier than anything he can move by himself. But because he wants to obey the Creator, he begins to push. *Surely God would create some way for me to move it,* he thinks to himself, or He wouldn't have told him to do this. So, the man pushes for several hours and for several days. He sweats and he gets tired, but he pushes some more. At the end of many days of pushing, the man gets frustrated. He has been pushing, waiting for a miracle, but he realizes the rock hasn't moved one single inch.

"*Why,* God? Why did you tell me to move this rock when You knew You wouldn't make it possible for me to do so?" he cries out loud. God answers: "My son, I never told you to *move* the rock. I only told you to *push* the rock. And since you have obeyed me, just look at you: Your arms are strong and defined. Your back has grown powerful, and your legs are muscular from being planted and driven into the ground. I have not wasted your time, my son. I have only prepared you for what is to come. Now I will remove the rock so you can go past it and begin your journey."

This story makes an important point: A lot of times we assume we're prepared for action. The story doesn't go into why God needed the man to build muscles in his arms, legs, and back, but it suggests that he can't accomplish his purpose without them. It has been placed on his heart and mind that he has a mission, but he doesn't realize what his mission is! Only when he begins a conversation with God does he realize that his assignment has nothing to do with the rock; the rock has only helped *prepare* him for his assignment.

When I use the phrase "conversation with God" in reference to beginning your journey into business ownership, I'm referring to a journey of quiet reflection about your professional and personal goals. When I decided I wanted to start BBF Engineering Services, I prayed about what I wanted. My main motivation didn't involve just *wanting to be my own boss.* My main motivation was to be able to control and manage the days I spent at home raising children, while growing professionally at the same time. I asked God for this because I had always wanted it for myself and my husband—to have a family life that allowed us both to contribute in ways that helped equally to meet our goals. I also wanted to be a mentor for my sons. Not just the person who kissed and hugged them hello and goodbye, but the person who showed them firsthand what they could accomplish in their lives.

Regardless of your spiritual beliefs, this pre-launch time of reflection is vital to moving forward. Everything we do reflects a greater level of quality when we start toward our achievements with clear minds. Similar to prayer, meditation can be another way of gaining clarity. Before or after doing research on your field of interest, the cost of starting your company, or the product you'd like to develop, you can find a quiet place to sit and think in silence. It has been said that prayer is talking and meditation is listening, so if you relax and listen in a way that lets you obtain clarity, energy, and positive thoughts and answers, it becomes a conversation without words. Where and when you choose to pray and meditate will vary according to your situation and schedule, but this should be a regular part of your routine before laying the actual groundwork of your launch or outlining a business plan. You'll feel more confident about your strategy after taking time to consider your big endeavor. *How long should you pray and meditate before getting into gear?* Nobody can tell you. The point is to do this until you have a sense of peace about it, then move forward.

Be careful to separate your sense of peace from your sense of eagerness. Feeling excited about your goal is healthy; rushing into what might be a major change for your life and your family is not. Start your conversation with God early in the process of making up your mind that running a business is what you definitely intend to do. Continue the conversation until you have calmness about it, a sense that your prayer and quiet time have allowed you some emotional distance from the dream you plan to pursue. It takes as long as it takes. Consider this your time of *pushing the rock,* but without all the sweating and grunting. Remember, the man in the story spent a long time pushing before God told him it was alright to walk ahead.

Another important thing to do while carrying on your conversation is *study.* Set aside separate time from your prayer and meditation to read books about achieving success and personal excellence. There's no time limit or requirement for when to complete the reading. In fact, it's good to have inspiring books you can refer to even when your business is up and running. The most inspiring book I have ever read is the Bible, the teaching and instruction of God. The teaching of the Word of God will help you prepare for your pursuits and leadership roles both in and out of the home.

The thing all good CEOs and leaders have in common is their ability to use general lessons about life and achievement in ways that benefit their businesses. A boss who knows how to get the job done, but doesn't know how to translate this wisdom to those who work for her, doesn't do any good for herself *or* the company. Similarly, a mate who knows what it takes to support a relationship, but doesn't demonstrate this knowledge by extending time and attention to his or her partner, sets up the relationship to fail.

Why do you think so many athletes make great players, but poor coaches? Because they know how to win, but they don't always know how to *teach* winning. They have to be able to motivate others, since they can't just magically give their own talents and skills to the team. In just about any sport, most players and coaches will agree that *heart* is the key element in succeeding. It's not always about who can run the fastest or jump the highest. Muhammad Ali, then called Cassius Clay, was barely out of his teens when he became the heavyweight boxing champion of the world. He didn't hit the hardest, but he still won by a knockout. He had heart!

As Scripture states in Proverbs, the race is not always won by the swift, nor the battle by the strong, but by the one who endures until the end. Translated to the competitive world, this statement means there is no greatness without heart and persistence. Developing the integrity and persistence to press on toward obtaining our purpose can be shown in our commitments to God, to our family, and to our business. My commitment to press forward was enhanced by praying and learning to inspire myself, even in the midst of a discouraging environment. We may sometimes have to look hard and deep for certain kinds of inspiration. This is the cost of moving to the next level of achievement, even if we've already done great things with our lives. The rewards are always worth the effort.

There's one last thing to consider after preparing yourself through conversation with God and others and study. This is optional, but it can be the final step in your mental conditioning for the journey ahead. Think of a person close to you who is, or has always been, a source of encouragement. Using outside support from friends or relatives, while not required, creates the feeling of a team approach.

Try to choose someone outside of the immediate family whom you hope will benefit from your business transition. It may very well be that your husband or child is the most encouraging person in your life. But the fair thing is to consider that everyone in your home will already be affected by the change you're about to make. They will already be witnessing every trial and challenge, and they may be prejudiced about some of their opinions and observations. Recruit a good friend or relative who won't be directly impacted by the effort you put into building your company and ask him or her to be your *vision partner*. Today there are professionals who call themselves "life coaches." Their business is helping to guide others toward their goals. They seek paying clients who need support in their achievements. Choosing a vision partner allows you the benefit of having someone in a role similar to that of a life coach, but without the formal training and without the cost. For the person you choose, there may be very little responsibility other than being available as a listener and giving honest feedback about your performance, whether in your efforts as family provider or business owner.

My early vision partners included my parents and my only brother, Renford. Unfortunately, my mother and my brother did not have the opportunity to see me start BBF Engineering Services. They never visited my office or read any of the nationally published magazine articles written about the company. As a matter of fact, my mom and brother probably didn't even realize their roles as my vision partners. Neither did I, as a young adult, because each of them played the role in a different way. My mother was the most caring, compassionate, and patient person I have met in my life thus far. Her ability to be a loving wife and mother was amazing, especially considering her lifelong adult battle with the disease of paranoid schizophrenia. I thank God for giving her the ability to teach me how to be a compassionate and loving wife and mother to my family in the midst of the struggles that life presents daily.

My brother Renford, whom we called "Tee," was killed in 1982. He had a difficult adult life after he returned from serving in the military during the Vietnam War. Even though he was a decorated soldier, who was awarded the Purple Heart and Bronze Star, his transition back into the civilian world was less than smooth. The one thing that remained constant about Tee, that I could always rely on, was his encouragement and support. I can still remember the way he would tell people his sister was a "genius" and how he'd talk to me about the great things I would do one day. A math whiz himself, Tee was the person who helped me with math when I was younger, and math would become a big part of my studies as I got into college and went forward with my engineering major. I was his youngest sister, and knowing he believed in me meant something even more special than having my parents' support. Tee made me feel like he would always be there if I needed him, like there was nothing in the world he wouldn't do to help me if it was within his reach.

You can imagine my devastation when I was notified that my only brother was murdered in September, 1982. I knew bad things happened to people every day, but it was the first time anything so violent and tragic had ever hit so close to home. Never again would I be able to count on Tee's encouragement or have him in my corner, where he'd stood cheering me on for so long. I began feeling my mortality. I started to question myself. I started to question the purpose of my existence. *If someone so close to me could be taken away in an instant, what was the value of going on?* I had started my senior year at Michigan State University in the college of engineering. I had been serious and focused when I came to school, but now I seriously thought about taking time off. I wanted to get away from my routine and reflect for awhile. Then it occurred to me: I was about to be thrown off course. Like anyone who loses a loved one, I needed time to grieve, but leaving school for an extended period would set me back more than necessary. Tee wouldn't have wanted this. In fact, he would have been disappointed in my decision. If I left school, I could be opening the door for making more bad decisions, therefore allowing a dramatic change in the destiny of my life. A lot of times when students leave school, they never return. I couldn't see myself letting Tee down after all the good he'd left behind in my life. It wouldn't have felt right. So, I stayed in school and I graduated on time.

In this sense, Tee was my absentee vision partner. He was never able to see the vision fulfilled, but it was his presence—first in the flesh and then in my memories—that helped me while I pushed toward my goals. This is the primary role of a vision partner. It doesn't take any unique qualifications or experience level to serve in that special capacity, but the person you choose should be able to care about your progress. That's all it takes. Whether you meet for coffee or lunch every day, or talk long-distance once a week, your choice of a vision partner should be someone who cares about you and your goals. It doesn't take a contract or even a handshake. All you have to do is express that you would like this person to be open to your conversation, concerns, and plans for your business and family whenever you need to discuss them.

What, then, is the difference between a vision partner and a friend? It's surely hard to imagine having a person play the role properly and be one of your worst enemies! Still, it can be filled by a person who is less personally involved with you, someone who may not even have any real connection with your private or social life. A former teacher or professor, for example, or even a coworker from the job you're leaving to start your company, can care enough to want to see you reach your professional goals. Make no mistake about it, a friend who can also help support your vision is beautiful. Hopefully you have the kinds of friends who do this anyway, but not all of them will be well-suited for the specific job I'm describing. Like family members, some of them may be too close to you to appreciate the sacrifices that having everything you want—truly *having it all*—may take. They may tell you to go back to your old job the first time you talk to them about an obstacle or a challenge in running your own company. Not that they don't mean well;

they would just rather see you happy than disappointed. But the last thing you'll want is a partner in your vision who keeps giving you reasons to let go of it.

Be certain to choose someone who can separate caring about your vision from caring about you. If this person can do both at the same time, it's all the better for you. He or she should be a good listener, someone who gives honest feedback when you need it. It goes without saying that trust in your vision partner is crucial. You should never have to worry that anything you want kept private, especially involving your business affairs, could be repeated. It has to be a mutually comfortable and casual sort of relationship in order for it to work. Ultimately, the hardest tasks will be yours to handle, but you just might find that after a conversation with God, it's pleasing to share what you heard with someone who cares.

"Have a Conversation with God."

SEVEN POWERFUL POINTERS

1. Pray about your business venture before beginning it and be sure to *Listen* to God for His revelation.

    a. Matthew 17:5
    b. Proverbs 2:6
    c. Proverbs 3:5

2. Read and study inspirational books that will help prepare you for your journey.

    a. Proverbs 4: 10–11
    b. Proverbs 19:20
    c. Proverbs 1:5
    d. Proverbs 2:5

3. Make a decision to move forward with fulfilling God's purpose for your life.

    a. Proverbs 2:20
    b. Proverbs 3:6

4. It takes *heart* and commitment, not just talent, to succeed.

    a. Proverbs 10:4

5. Consider finding a *vision partner* who will help keep you focused.

    a. Proverbs 8:14
    b. Proverbs 8:33
    c. Proverbs 11:14

6. Learn to apply life-lessons to the way you'll run your company.

   a. Proverbs 28:14
   b. Proverbs 29:12
   c. Proverbs 29:18
   d. 1 Thessalonians 4:6

7. Develop a reputation for being one who conducts business and personal affairs with integrity, good character, and ethical behavior. Don't be a moral coward!

   a. Leviticus 19:11
   b. Proverbs 4:14
   c. Proverbs 6: 16–19
   d. Proverbs 10:6
   e. Proverbs 19:1

IDENTIFY YOUR PASSION
AND YOUR PURPOSE

By a certain age it is easy for most of us, as adults, to say what we want out of our careers and professional experience. It takes us all different amounts of time, and we arrive at these decisions from different directions. Yet at some point, if we've properly examined our passion and purpose, most of us feel pretty confident in declaring our chosen vocation. At times we'll change our minds and decide upon a different path, but the initial identification of our purpose should be a deliberate process that is not rushed.

I have a talent and a passion for being a barber, and at one point in my life I considered going to barber school. Imagine how different my career might have been if I'd opened the BBF Barbershop instead of BBF Engineering Services. What I think helped move me more toward my current career was the greater pull of my purpose. My *purpose* was given to me directly through prayer and meditation. You should always pursue the business venture that is most rooted in your passion *and* your purpose. In my case, engineering is what fit these criteria.

After you've meditated on your professional goals, you should have a clear idea of what fits these for you. Determine your purpose and then determine your passion. The process for determining these has to be an act of reflection and careful consideration. Should they be a purpose and passion that are geared toward working with other people and touching their lives? For example, starting a restaurant or going into the hair and manicuring business? Your passion might be something that would allow you to speak into people's lives. There are numerous books that discuss ways to find your purpose, and career counseling can be found at the adult vocational and community centers located in most cities.

Even the local unemployment agency will often provide some direction with testing and identifying skill sets that help indicate professional purpose. There are various ways for you to go about determining what you're best qualified to do, and you'll already know pretty well what it is that you *enjoy* doing—i.e., your passion. There are even personality tests that can be good indicators of purpose. What do people say about you? Do your friends and family tell you how clever and funny you are? Do you make people laugh without trying? Are you able to brighten people's days by making them smile? Maybe that means you should consider a career in comedy. "But I'm really shy in front of crowds," you say. Well, you can still make that work for your personality. Your purpose might be to start your own production company and write hilarious stage plays and television shows. Nothing should be considered out of reach or too ambitious.

But there's a difference between your purpose and your personality, and you have to remember that. Your personality is what determines how you relate to and interact with others from a very tender age. Your purpose is often shaped to fit your personality. Your passion comes into play largely as a result of your personality and your purpose growing in sync with one another. But they won't always be the same. Your passion may be playing basketball. Earvin "Magic" Johnson, as a result of his outgoing and competitive personality and his enormous talent, was a five-time champion with the Los Angeles Lakers, and he was also the team captain. Having won championships since he was a teenager, his purpose was obviously to be a team leader. But when he retired from basketball, first due to the concern that HIV would affect his health and ability to perform on the court, and then to focus on other areas of interest, it became clear that he had a purpose beyond basketball, even though basketball had been his passion since his growing-up years in Lansing, Michigan. He then branched off into some of the most successful entrepreneurial endeavors that any of today's businessmen have ever undertaken, including: movie theaters, Starbuck's coffee houses, and a popular record label. So, while his passion was always playing basketball, his larger *purpose* was to serve the urban communities where he brought new jobs and businesses and to begin serving as an example of how broadly natural leaders can expand their leadership skills.

When your passion and purpose don't necessarily line up, it's not always a bad thing. But many times people, in this case, are unhappy. Depending on what life-stage you're in, your situation may dictate that you have to wait on pursuing your passion. Maybe it's volunteering at a hospital, but you've got kids and mouths to feed, so your main purpose for the moment must be providing for them. You *can* pursue both your purpose and your passion at different times. Sometimes that's necessary, because within your purpose there are different seasons. There are some who live out their purpose in life early on, but from what I've seen the majority of people have to walk through life's "prep school" of hard knocks, experience relationships, and become obedient to God before they have the privilege of working toward it.

I've observed that people who wait until long after the prime of life to live out their purpose were not obedient to pursuing their purpose when they were younger. That's not to say it's too late, but they will often say, "I'm too old," or, "It's too late." If they say that enough, they'll begin to believe it, and lose the courage to pursue their life's purpose.

In the beginning you might be fortunate enough to have people tell you, "No it's not…No, you're not." But they're not going to do that for twenty years! Nobody's going to stay at your *pity party* forever. It's wise to try and allow things in your life to happen in the right order. If you have a child before you're ready, it can take you off course. Or, you might marry the wrong person and the marriage ends up in a divorce. It takes you off course. Realize early that the decisions you make can alter the destiny planned for your life. In the end, however, channeling your energy toward your life's purpose is still possible, even up to the end of your days. It's been done many times—but the idea is to try and make obedient choices that reflect it from the outset.

Across the years I've tried to be in tune to what I felt I needed to do to stay *proactive,* instead of *reactive,* so I could have the proper goal elements in place when the time was right for me to use them. Probably my biggest mistakes were made in relationships before I got married. I didn't go through abuse or anything so terrible, but I made some wrong choices in men, and those choices could have been missteps that changed my future. Fortunately, they didn't take me so far off track I wasn't able to get refocused on the life and family I knew I wanted one day.

Your business purpose may reveal more of itself after you've had the appropriate experience and training while pursuing a passion. In my case, I do not make my living as a writer, but I felt that part of my purpose was to help provide some inspiration and guidance through this book for other people pursuing their dreams. My passion and entrepreneurial purpose fifteen years ago was different than it is now. Often, your main purpose depends on what *season* of life you're in. People who have adult sons and daughters may have enough money saved in the bank that they don't worry about the same things as younger people with a mortgage, bills, and babies.

Your Creator wants you to have the desires of your heart, but you must maintain an attitude of forward thinking and persistence toward making the right steps in the pursuit to accomplish your desires and goals. In our eyes, some celebrities seem to have the greatest success, success we could never imagine for ourselves. But it's all relative to the individual. The celebrities we watch on TV who have lots and lots of money don't always have the successful family life that you may have. They may not have close friends they can trust or expect to be around when their star starts to fade. Even the most powerful, wealthiest celebrity may desire something another person has, no matter how common it seems, or how much the person who *has* it may take it for granted.

Along with passion and purpose, there are other personal things to consider in your readiness to start your business, like *where* you should conduct it. Eight years after starting my business, I expanded from my home because I needed a sense of physical separation for the business, and my children were now both in school full-time. For professional appearance and the fact that, between the home and the office, you may have difficulty separating work from home commitments, the separation may become necessary. When you have meetings and professional appointments, you don't want to have them at your house; rather, at an office. At some point, separate the home base from the work base so you can keep your sanity and determine how many hours a day you're working on the business, compared with hours devoted to your family.

The majority of my company staff are located at field sites, but with office-based staff, like receptionists or bookkeepers, you would not place them in your home office. If you have a legitimate home-based business, you can write off the portion of home expenses that you devote to business use, so there's a tax advantage here, but at what point does it become inconvenient to stay located in the home? My home office situation got to the point where I'd look up and my husband would be sitting at my computer, and I'd say, "Mike, I've got some work to do." He'd say, "I'll be off in a minute," and it might be an hour before he was finished. That didn't work for me—or for him, either. Growing pains can be good as they indicate the need to change and expand.

You should also consider the concept of a "virtual office." For example, I had a corporate address where I would only have meetings. It wasn't staffed and it wasn't particularly important that I go there daily to complete my work. *Is it really necessary to be involved in dealing back and forth between clients and children, or is it time to move the business out of your home completely? Is being in your home even starting to hinder the growth of your business?* These are questions you should revisit and answer as your business grows.

Another consideration along these same lines, which also extends to purpose and passion for entrepreneurs, is franchising. Any number of successful business leaders earn a living and support their families by buying into national or international corporate chains and outlets. Everything from a gas station to a cosmetics carrier or a legal service agency can fall under the banner of franchise ownership. When you become the subsidiary of a parent company you're a *franchisee,* and a lot of times you don't necessarily need to move out of your home to become one. Except for the ones maintained by the founders of McDonald's, all of the other thousands and thousands of McDonald's restaurants are franchises licensed to operate, but not solely or fully owned businesses. Likewise, there are art dealers (working through parent companies) that sell portraits and sculptures to decorate homes and offices.

These dealers can work flexibly and can successfully operate as their own bosses, according to the specifications and guidelines detailing how their parent organization allows them to do this. Franchises will typically determine *where* you can open your business and whether you need a specific building space and configuration. This can be a happy medium for those who want to do something in between leaving the payroll of a company and going into business entirely for themselves. Franchising eliminates a lot of the creative work involved with building a company from the ground up, but it also restricts the amount of growth, freedom, and satisfaction that can be experienced by the franchisee. Still, if you have a purpose that leads you into business ownership and a passion for operating one, there is always the franchising alternative. It's even possible for a franchise owner to gain valuable experience by working in the area of his or her passion while maintaining a full-time job, which can serve as necessary training before the entrepreneur goes out completely on his or her own.

Once you have successfully thought out and prayed over what your vision will be, you have one key step left before launching your enterprise: Make sure your training and your business vision match your ambitions.

I recommend a minimum of five years of applicable work experience or training in your chosen field prior to entertaining the idea of branching out as an entrepreneur. Many of you have probably already been working in your industry, while others have been going to college in the evening after work. Still others have made the choice to do just what you enjoy during off hours and weekends, without ever trying to turn it into a career. Regardless of the stage you're in, you'll still need to apply every lesson you've learned in the first guideline to gain the focus needed at this pre-launch point. It wouldn't serve any purpose for you to dive headfirst into a five-year journey toward a goal you never researched, or achieved the proper peace and mental preparation to pursue. Neither would it be fair to take time and attention away from your family and waste it going through the motions of a goal you haven't fully considered or committed yourself toward reaching.

Don't overlook the gift of opportunity and the favor of God. Weigh the options and think about things like how much money you've got saved, how much business you're getting, and how quitting your regular job would affect your family. Find out if you can take a leave of absence while you launch your business, rather than prematurely resigning. Remember that *someone* in your household should serve as a source of stable income. One of the main points of this guideline is that you can't achieve what you're setting out to do without obtaining the knowledge required to have the potential for the highest level of success.

Having the basic qualifications necessary to succeed in your new career is essential. Having the vision without the skill to support it is a downfall of many new business owners. Think about it. How many times have you seen a small store or company open for a year or less, and then close its doors? Usually you'll hear an explanation like, "Business was slow." Slow business is never the disease; it's just the symptom. *Why* was business so slow? The answer to this question is directly related to skill support. Whether the skill was money management, marketing, or product selection, it was a skill issue. The vision may have been a powerful one that could have changed the business owner's life and a lot of others. If skill wasn't properly considered, the vision was doomed from the beginning.

Skill comes primarily from experience. You can be a talented individual who is born with certain gifts. Maybe you've been a wonderful singer for as long as you can remember. This is an example of God-given talent, not of skill. Skill comes from developing your talent. If you sing beautifully, but don't know how to use your vocal range to hit the proper notes, you're still lacking something important. You'll sound so awkward in the church choir that people will pray for you to be quiet! That makes you no less of a great singer; you're just a singer who lacked the proper development of skills—a singer who never achieved maximum potential.

Your career goal may already dictate the requirement of time you'll invest in preparing and the skills you'll develop to succeed. Thinking about starting your own law firm? Well, of course this means that you'll spend years in law school, and then you'll have to pass the bar examination for the state(s) where you intend to practice. It's not much different for doctors than for engineers and other professionals who make careers by using the at-large public, rather than specific segments, as their clientele. They are held to different legal and governing standards for self-employment than those who make a living providing goods and services. We may not always think of them as entrepreneurs, but they have the option of seeking positions with other agencies and organizations, just like everyone else. Their requirements shouldn't lead you to think you've got it any easier that a doctor or lawyer. Take your cake baking or house painting just as seriously as you would want your dentist to take cleaning your teeth. The idea is to put all the things in place that you'll need to operate in your field of expertise without having to totally depend on other people to start you on your road to success.

I had to obtain a certain amount of professional experience in order to start my company, along with fulfilling licensing and certification requirements to operate as a project consultant and an engineering corporation. I would never have been awarded state contracts to inspect major freeways just by getting my engineering degree. I would have had to get on board with another professional who had the accreditation I did not have, and even if that person accepted me as a partner and a business peer, I'd still be unable to operate the company as the sole shareholder. I would risk losing the ability to operate the business if we ever had a parting of the ways. You don't want to put yourself in that kind of position. It might be true that you're just as smart as or smarter than the other person, but you may never have the chance to prove it if you can't call your own shots.

Building a resume of experience and qualifications in whatever area you operate will increase your abilities, along with the customer's faith in your company. You may have to work part-time, in addition to your regular job, just to gain experience in the industry where you plan to open your business. Again, you could request a leave of absence to facilitate your launch. You might consider adjusting your schedule to work evenings, if your primary job allows it, so you can take day courses in the field where your goal awaits.

There are many possible approaches, so give this time and thought. Can you afford to reduce your work hours and devote extra time to learning what you need to learn? Don't shrink away from volunteering, offering your time and energy free of charge, in exchange for a chance to learn the business. It's hard to imagine any smart boss who won't accept some form of apprentice work that doesn't require a paycheck. It may be that you're only allowed to make coffee, deliver faxes, and sit in on staff meetings, but it lets you observe without being a real threat in the form of competition to the company.

It's always easier to add these types of changes to your routine, and especially to your financial budget, if you've got help at home. Single parents launching a new business would be smart to establish a savings account beforehand to meet future financial expenses, because they can expect smaller paychecks for a while and added childcare costs. Remember to think it through before starting, and make decisions that produce financial *life,* not death!

"Identify Your Passion and Your Purpose."

SEVEN POWERFUL POINTERS

1. Choose a business that is in line with your purpose and passion.

   a. Proverbs 20:18
   b. Ecclesiastes 3:1
   c. Ecclesiastes 3:17

2. Personality and passion can combine to reveal purpose.

   a. Romans 8:28
   b. Romans 9:11
   c. Romans 9:17

3. Along with purpose and passion, consider location in preparing to start a business.

   a. 1 Samuel 21:2

4. Franchising is a possible alternative to private ownership.

   a. Acts 6:3–4

5. Research the educational and legal requirements of the business you are pursuing.

   a. Romans 12:11

6. Make sure you obtain the skills you need to launch your business.

   a. Proverbs 22:29

7. Strive to make decisions that produce life results, not death.

   a. Proverbs 3:1–2
   b. Proverbs 8:36
   c. Proverbs 10:16
   d. Proverbs 18:21

BE RESOURCEFUL AND REFINE YOUR VISION

Have you heard the business saying that your value is found in the numbers on your contact lists? Well, this applies equally at work and at home. It doesn't always literally refer to telephone numbers on your personal digital assistant (PDA) and cellular phone, either. Sometimes it will, but the way this idea pertains most to your home and business experience is that it reveals how you involve others as resources for support and networking.

Being a *resourceful* husband or wife, parent, and business owner will be a top requirement from the very beginning of your road to success. Knowing whom to call and where to call to add the services and supplements to your home and company settings will always put you ahead of the game. It will also make you a wiser leader than those who struggle or burn out because they never learned how to delegate responsibility. Being a good leader in and outside of your home means knowing when to call in reinforcements.

One form of reinforcement that will always be needed to help you manage both your home and career is money. Every family won't be able to spare their savings to support the individual ventures of one member. It's sad to say that entire households have been ruined when a person squandered the finances that were needed for the everyday support of all. You can research the various government and private agencies that offer monetary support for entrepreneurs at your local library and through the Internet. Important business-related information about resources is also available through educational and philanthropic programs.

Interning and apprenticeships are immensely valuable experiences in preparing you for a career—even more so than when I was a college student and engineering intern more than twenty years ago. Professional competition is steadily increasing and technologies rapidly changing. It's a sign of the times that on-the-job learning is a great deal more valuable than book knowledge. It is increasingly true that there are full-time moms returning to school and other experienced workers who find they must undergo beginner's training when following new career paths. These sought after positions may not be truly entry-level positions, but a certain degree of experience, in one form or another, is required for serious consideration by employers. Medical students have to complete hospital residency requirements. Journalism students need newsroom experience at radio and television stations. The blue-collar labor jobs, like construction, will even look at a new recruit's track record with projects, as opposed to just asking if he or she has read and learned only the standard safety procedures.

On the other hand, when it comes to family considerations, there's no real distinction made between the long-time, well-paid employee and the intern-apprentice. In most cases, those forty-year-old moms who decide to return to college don't get cut any slack on caring for their children, no matter what it takes. Whether they're paid a little for interning or no salary at all, the company that hires them views it as an opportunity for the intern. There's often no guarantee that an apprentice will be hired full-time. That leaves interns having to pay bills and find babysitters without the promise of support from supervisors. Ideally, the person best suited for this sort of arrangement is probably a childless student attending college on a tuition-paid, all-expense scholarship. But the number of full-ride scholarship students is itself a relatively small one, frequently made up of athletes, so the vast majority of interns just have to make the best of their individual circumstances. This might involve taking a primary job for pay, raising a family, attending classes, and training as an intern—all at the same time.

Careful time management is the only way to survive. Nobody said it would be easy, but it's the way things are; because, believe me, if you make a poor impression as an intern, it will count against you. You're not being recruited just to take up space and, usually, not only because employers want to be nice and take you under their wing. They expect the same level of commitment from trainees that's expected from veterans, and if they don't see it there's a problem. Depending on the supervisor, you may not ever know there is an issue until you receive a poor evaluation. Even worse, you may be denied the positive professional recommendation letter or other formal credit you hoped to earn by interning in the first place.

The next thing to do after you've completed your training is to refine the vision of your new enterprise. Through your training and preparation time you should not only get as much knowledge as possible, but you should also explore as many options as your field presents. For example, in the legal arena there are *criminal law* and *business law* focuses, and within those categories are various areas of focus that range from *public defending* to *negotiating* million-dollar contracts. The same goes for the culinary arts. There's a different discipline involved with baking cakes and pastries than with meal planning as a chef at a restaurant or working in a hospital as a nutritionist. Business opportunities will reveal themselves more clearly as you immerse yourself in training. There are multiple paths to the same goal in the process of owning a company, even when your field has been chosen.

One of the worst mistakes you can make is pouring your time and money into a business that leaves you unfulfilled. You might as well have kept your old job! Focusing on regrets that you didn't consider the best angle for approaching your goal will be a distraction that's costly in more ways than just the obvious ones. In some cases it's possible to simply expand the range of your services. But be careful not to expand so much that the customer gets a feeling you're not good at any one thing, or that they could get more value from hiring a specialist. There are clients who feel most comforted by the knowledge that when they hire a company it *specializes* in only the area where their need lies.

The most educated customers will have learned the differences between functions at a company that offers more than one service. He or she may be particularly concerned about whether there is a clear enough separation of duties among the company's personnel. It's kind of like walking into a dollar store to buy trash bags. We might notice that the store also sells light bulbs, Christmas cards, candy bars, and soap. But what happens when we look over and see an item that we would never feel comfortable buying from the dollar store? Like, let's say, jewelry. Just imagine the conversation on Valentine's Day:

Woman: Honey, I've never seen such an unusual necklace. You must have spent a fortune!
Man: No, I got it at a great price.
Woman: It's just so beautiful! Where did you ever find it?
Man: Over at Dan's Dollar Dynasty.
Woman: (*Begins choking him with the necklace.*)

This is not to suggest that most of us wouldn't know the difference between cheap jewelry and the real thing. The point is that not everyone is comfortable with a one-stop-shop mentality.

Customers always want to know that we really "specialize" in our specialty. So, it's best to have considered as many choices as are available before beginning your business, rather than trying to work backwards to create a multipurpose company because you don't enjoy your career. Sometimes, despite our best intentions, things veer off in different directions for us, personally and professionally. All the planning, outlining, and considering in the world won't prevent an occasional bad call or unforeseeable circumstance. A bad experience with a demanding client might make you wish you had gone into consulting rather than staff recruitment and training, even though both are in the field of human resources. A human resource degree would never have prepared you for the sort of problem you might encounter. It would only educate you about the science and strategies involved. And, serving as a clerk or assistant at a staffing agency, even if it provided valuable hands-on experience, wouldn't prepare you for dealing with tough clients who only complained to the boss about their issues.

So, your passion for working with people and helping to match them with the right job opportunities would be a good fit with your experience. Unfortunately it wouldn't prepare you to become the main person on the firing line when you went out to do seminars and group sessions to coach employees about entering the marketplace. Understandably, you could decide that you don't enjoy training and you would rather focus on building resumes and business portfolios for customers. A lot of this can be done through the Internet and may still leave you with the sense of fulfillment that you get from leading seminars. In this case, there would be no deficiency in the planning stages where you went wrong, and if there's no major loss of income or waste of resources that were needed to get your company up and running, you avoid a setback. Don't beat yourself up if you *do* find yourself in a situation like this one after doing your best to avoid it. Far more often than not, when you explore your options and *then* make your best move, you will avoid the experience of feeling regret later.

One good way to think about it is this: Lawyers go into battle, while judges control the action. Think about your options from that perspective, because this applies across the span of careers. Will you be the judge, a lawyer, or maybe even *both* when running your company? This is a time when all of the decisions will be yours to make.

Household support outlets are just as important for you and your family as business and education supports to your company. The mother is the one who typically spends the most time with the children, so I have learned to create activities that my husband and our children can do together. I schedule activities for my husband and children to enjoy together that include common interests. That's how it works in my house, because I want my husband to have his own bonding time with the boys. When you're a mom who handles most of the children's arrangements, or if you happen to be a dad who is the more hands-on parent, a little planning on your part can help ensure regular, quality interaction between the children and the other parent. Naturally, there are households where the men may need to take this advice more than the women. Still, the opportunities for interaction and resources that support the children will generally be the same, ranging from trips to the local athletic center for various programming to organized recreation.

Typically I don't have each of my children involved in more than one team sport at a time. Basketball, football, baseball, and soccer all require practice to properly introduce kids to the concept of teamwork. I don't worry so much about an activity like karate if I'm trying to keep the children's schedule manageable, because their attendance at individual classes is more flexible. The baseball team typically meets twice a week. If you are out of the house every evening of the week with scheduled children's activities, this adds to your obligations and makes your days longer, but individual activities like music lessons, martial arts, or exercise classes are not usually so time-consuming for the parents. The pace and the structure of the practice and training is often more flexible.

For example, my children have piano lessons at home, which is more convenient than when I took them outside of our home to their lessons. One of the greatest challenges in harmonizing your business life with your family life is taking great care about the influences that you allow within your home, no matter how busy your schedule becomes. I agree with the conventional wisdom that you should monitor what you let children watch on television and the extent of the exposure and images you allow to be delivered to them. Too often, parents make the mistake of neglecting real character-building resource activities for children in favor of planting them in front of a television. Many households share the anything–that–keeps–them–quiet philosophy, and this is particularly tempting for those who have working space at home, but it's dangerous if we don't know *what* has their attention.

You may live in one of the households where the television is on all the time, but when you have children you should expect that there's going to be a lifestyle change. Some of the things you *were* able to do when childless you're not going to be able to do anymore, and that should be acknowledged and embraced. But be mindful of the best ways to incorporate replacements. If it's not an improvement, you may as well leave it alone. When you hire babysitters, make sure you choose people and environments that are going to have positive impacts on the children's lives, not just those who are available and convenient.

People say you can't control who your children are going to be around, but you can. And that doesn't mean choosing their friends for them. It means being conscious and discriminating about the environments in which you let them choose playmates and close acquaintances. Do your best to select the schools, churches, and neighborhoods that provide the best environments for your family. Any adults allowed in their presence should be a person you know and approve of in terms of their moral and ethical character. Pray for discernment about the *real* character of people and always give attention to your innermost feelings. You know, a lot of times people grow up and they have all kinds of problems, and you realize the reason is because they were influenced by some adult they shouldn't have been around in the first place!

I've had an example or two of that in my own family. Fortunately my parents were great judges of character, so there were adults we were never allowed to be alone with as children. Parents need to have the ability and desire to discern negative character traits in adults when determining the family relationships. It's one thing to trust yourself with another adult, but it's another thing to leave an innocent child with someone or in some situation that might be dangerous for them, because there's no erasing the physical or emotional damage once something happens. When my children are home we allow them to watch age-appropriate television on a time-limited basis. We take careful consideration as to the language or whether the program has elements of witchcraft or sorcery, which is against our personal value system.

We may have to make special provisions to be sure we don't let certain influences into our homes, directly or indirectly. A friend of your children who's used to hearing a lot unfavorable language and discussions in his or her household could come over to play and think it's normal to hear that language in every home. You don't necessarily want to stop your child from associating with that friend, but you *do* want to consider the type and degree of interaction between your child and that child. Keep all relationships in perspective, such that your home environment remains one of peacefulness for your family and for those whom you allow to enter your home. Your family will appreciate it if their home represents a place of solace and peace—a true feeling of home!

It's important to establish the order and peace of your home if you're planning to launch into a career change like owning a business. If you're too busy dealing with household problems and issues, or if you're unprepared, you won't have time to work on the business when the opportunity arrives, anyway. As it pertains to your family's potential gain, the focus of your business should be on helping to save and prepare for their future. There are other legacies, besides money, that you can create for your mate and children while you travel this journey. My dad left us the legacy of hard work and the importance of education, while my mother left a legacy of motherly compassion and the unselfish desire to serve others. It's important to make sure that whatever legacy you leave your family by going into business isn't a financially or mentally damaging one.

Children should see things in both parents that will make them proud. It's good for them to observe a family mentoring process. What my boys see in their dad is a man who is providing them with a disciplined, responsible example of a man with good character and integrity. What they see in me is the love of a strong mother who is also a small business entrepreneur. What they see between the two of us are parents who love one another and are committed to the covenant of marriage.

It's good to take opportunities on Career Day and similar events at the children's school to go in and talk about your business. You make your children proud and give them a sense of what it's like to be the boss at work. I can remember when my oldest son was on this venture where anyplace we went and he saw an employee, he would ask, "Are you the boss?" He had come to appreciate the idea of being a leader by watching me lead my company. It's also a smart idea to participate in "Take Your Child to Work Day" whenever the schools and communities you live in observe this. It has been fairly popular among parents who go to their jobs and allow their sons and daughters to observe them while on the clock. Some teachers will want the children to write a report or essay about the experience. Imagine what your son or daughter can share with the class after going to a business that you own and operate. Imagine how your child's observations will stand out from the others!

Don't go into business for yourself so you can slack off on your work and be lazy without having a boss to answer to for it. Your children will notice the change in your work habits. A lot of parents let their children stay home from school frequently. Kids who are taught it's alright to be that way grow up to be adults who think it's alright to be that way. I happened to like school when I was a child. I even wanted to attend school when I was ill in order to avoid getting behind and having to make up work. This is in addition to the fact that my parents wouldn't go for my waking up and saying I didn't want to go to school, if nothing was seriously wrong with me. Though I did not come from an immediate family of entrepreneurs, it is the life lessons, such as my desire and drive to press forward through various circumstances, that helped me to overcome the negative comments and limiting actions of cynics. My family legacy of education, hard work, and desire to serve were instrumental in creating an environment of success.

No one's going to give you a contract to do things you're not qualified to do, so I had to work hard to establish myself, since there was no money or family business for me to inherit and take over. When you're traveling the path that God has set for you, negative influences will be removed from your life, because they turn your attention away from your purpose. If you're a mechanic and you do your job well and give fair prices, maybe that's your ministry, but you don't necessarily want to own the garage. Then again, it may be in your future to open a chain of service stations. Sometimes it's the *inner push* you must give yourself to force yourself to find and follow the right paths when you don't have the upbringing to prepare you to do so.

It's a testament in itself that most of the successful business owners I know had a positive home upbringing, but where that stability was missing you have to find outside support and keep a focus on improving, so that you can break the cycle and preserve an opportunity to help your own family in the future. In every case, if you're not behaving with honor, love, and respect toward the people who work with you, for you, and around you, you weaken the structure and foundation of your company—but especially if the company is based at home. For many people, there is the attractive option of establishing an actual family-owned business. What better resources are there for a business than the people we know and trust? This can extend outside of the traditional home and include cousins, nieces, or siblings.

If funding is required to start your company, unless it's a gift, I don't advise accepting it. If you do accept funding, whether the funds are a loan or a gift, make sure you receive it accompanied by a contract or promissory note, even if it's from a sister, brother, or your best friend. People do strange things when you become successful, so you want to have a written record of the terms for any business agreement. You can seek outside investors, as another option, or shareholders, but then they become partners in the business, whether "silent partners" or those who are active in the administration. If someone wanted to become a partner in BBF Engineering Services, the requirement would be that they come up with the required funds to buy into the company. If you're a startup and you're receiving any kind of financial support from another business, it usually means you're starting out with a partner. The best plan is to save your money and use the funds you require to start *your* business.

An investor, partner, or silent partner will sometimes be recruited to provide financial support and guidance to a new business. Investors will expect a return in profits or shares of the business, while a partner may have a say in the day to day operations, in addition to expecting a return on their investment. I'm not an advocate of partnerships because I've seen too many partnerships turn out like bad marriages. But for every story of disappointment or failure, there's a story of success created out of similar circumstances. Before accepting any form of financial resources from individual investors or companies, sit down with your attorney and review the contractual obligations of the affected parties.

Lastly, among professional resources, whether it helps with hiring referrals, client recommendations, or other membership benefits, it's always good to consider affiliation with a professional organization that is relative to your area of expertise. The Better Business Bureau is a widely known agency that lists small and independent businesses, along with others having good community standing, but professional networks and organizations tend to allow for more interaction. Attending professional conferences and obtaining organizational newsletters can be helpful, especially when you're just starting out. It's always good to have a colleague to call or a website to visit if there is basic information about problems or changes in the industry that you're encountering. Most large professional agencies have state or city chapter affiliations that entitle a business to the same benefits as those throughout the country or the world.

"Be Resourceful and Refine Your Vision."

SEVEN POWERFUL POINTERS

1. Being a good leader means knowing when to call in reinforcements.

   a. Isaiah 42:16
   b. Isaiah 48:17

2. Involve children with both parents in leisure time.

   a. 2 Corinthians 12:14–15

3. Maintain your business focus on your area of expertise. Make sure clients are informed of your area of expertise.

   a. Leviticus 26:9
   b. Psalms 138:6

4. Get all formal business agreements in writing.

   a. Acts 6:3
   b. Romans 12:17
   c. 2 Corinthians 13:7

5. Look for creative ways to obtain training without hurting your home life.

   a. Proverbs 20:7

6. Be the type of boss who conducts business with excellent integrity, morals, and character.

   a. 1 Kings 9:4
   b. Psalms 19:1
   c. Psalms 25:21

7. Don't let your vision become so ambitious that you're missing what you're best at doing.

   a. Psalms 89:18–19
   b. Proverbs 11:3

LEARN WHAT PART YOU SHOULD PLAY

Remember the last time you saw a really good movie? Maybe you had some popcorn, shared a soda with your significant other, and laughed or talked about the film all the way home. Now imagine yourself back at the same theater on that same pleasant evening, watching that same enjoyable film. But add sticky floors—the kind that stick to your shoes because of drinks spilled on the floor. Throw in a projector that slips in and out of focus. And imagine yourself watching this film while you sit in really uncomfortable chairs.

Now, remember that you really enjoyed the movie. Chances are, however, that no matter how well you liked it, the unclean floor, worn seats, and defective projector would have taken away a lot from your experience. These kinds of problems would mean someone hasn't taken care of their responsibilities. The cleaning staff neglected the floor, the projector operator neglected his equipment, and maintenance paid no attention to the old, hard chairs. They hadn't learned their parts. It's easy to say they were just lazy or they knew their parts but failed to play them well. But it's more likely that those staffers missed a bigger part of their assignment than just the doing the work. They have failed to recognize the importance of their role.

Think of your product or service as an Academy Award-winning movie. You are the director and your staff, contractors, and business resources are your cast of characters and crew. The customers are your audience. By learning what part you play, you can strengthen everyone else's performance and increase the chances that audience members will talk about how great your picture was. It might sound a little easier than it is. Of course, in your own business you'll play the part of the president or chief executive officer—the boss. Nobody wants to start building a vision from the ground floor up, just to hand it over to someone else. But the role you take on as your own boss is crucial to the success of your business. Just because you *can* do everything, it doesn't mean that you *should.*

There are times when you may feel more qualified than everyone around you to do every job there is. This is a natural feeling that comes from the fact that you've known how you envisioned your enterprise and the way it should function better than anyone else. Acting on this feeling, on the other hand, is one of the biggest mistakes you could make right out of the gate. Be realistic. While many of us are multitalented, none of us does everything well. So, in learning what part you should play, it's good to start by listing on paper the team members you'll need to support your business plan. Even if you intend to start as a one-man or one-woman operation, you should, at least, consider who might help you with an occasional professional service. For example, accounting is a valuable service that everyone isn't qualified to provide. If you set out to become a carpenter and you plan to take on jobs that would require only your own manpower, it can't hurt to keep in touch with a person who will review your books periodically. This can help you to determine business growth trends that you may not have recognized because you're so busy promoting the company and seeking carpentry assignments. *Growth trends* are what help you determine when it may be time to expand and hire an assistant or a crew.

But for others who know from the start that they'll need employee support, learning the part to play helps to better establish the team's direction. Any good boss knows that hiring good people makes him or her look good. So ask yourself, "Who might handle this assignment better than I could handle it?" If you're a behind-the-scenes boss, it doesn't make you any less of a boss. Maybe instead of handling the sales and marketing of your company you'll want your main task to be internal supervision. That means you'll need to recruit a sales and marketing person to go out and be the face of your company. This person may do anything from writing brochures that promote the business to setting up client meetings. If you recognize that your greatest talent and passion is at a desk in front of a computer, that's the part you should play. Think about it in the historical sense. Martin Luther King and the civil rights activists needed a woman of color to sit down on the bus in Montgomery, Alabama. Rosa Parks was the person who started the protest against segregated transportation when she refused to give up her seat in 1955. But Dr. King was the leader, or *boss,* of that movement. I am so thankful that these individuals were willing and courageous in the parts they were each destined to play in the Civil Rights Movement that affects life as we know it today—all over the world!

Who would have ever thought that Betty Crocker, once voted the most famous woman in the country after Eleanor Roosevelt, never even existed? We've all heard of her baking products and cookbooks and have brought them into our kitchens at one time or another. She had to have lived, right? Only in the minds of executives at the Washburn Crosby Co., who learned their roles well. Members of that company, which later became General Mills, recognized that none of them would be as effective representing cooking products as a woman with a friendly face and a common name. A star was born. They even hired actresses to play Betty on a television show that taught celebrities how to bake. The name and face of Betty Crocker helped make their company a force in the food industry. Today, Betty Crocker's face doesn't appear on cake mixes and other products the way it did more than half-a-century ago, yet the brand name can be found in almost every supermarket. Imagine if some fellow called Benny Crocker had decided his name and face should be on the products because he was the boss. You get the idea: Learn what part you should play.

A major factor that should be obvious, but is sometimes overlooked in the learning of roles, is experience. I recommend a minimum of five years practice or training in your chosen field. I can hear you saying to yourself, "*Now* she tells me!" Yet, you should definitely not be discouraged by that advice if you've already read this far, because some of you have probably already been working in your industry. Others have been going to college in the evenings after work, or maybe just doing what you've enjoyed during off hours and weekends, without ever trying to turn it into a career. Regardless of the stage you're in, you'll still need to apply every lesson you've learned in the first guideline to gain the focus needed at this point. It wouldn't serve any purpose for you to dive headfirst into a five-year journey toward a goal you never researched or achieved the proper peace and mental preparation to pursue. Neither would it be fair to take time and attention away from your family and waste it going through the motions of a goal you haven't fully considered or committed yourself toward reaching. Still, keep in mind that circumstances will always vary.

Two years of interning at a nationally known computer technology company might be better preparation for a business owner than five years of studying the subject at a college. If you want to start a private investigator's agency, it could take only months to get the required licensing. If you've gained a reputation and customer base for building and selling doghouses when you're not working at the post office, and a friend offers you free space to open full-time, don't say, "Dr. Foster told me to wait five years!" The main point of this guideline is that you can't choose what part to play without the knowledge required for that part.

Being creative is a common trait among business leaders, and the single-parent entrepreneur may get even more practice in creative planning and strategy than the average person. Single or married, just as when you've finally gotten your business up and running, the trick will be for you to manage all the regular duties of home while you prepare. This will be a good testing ground for you to gauge what adjustments might have to be made in your schedule when the day arrives that you open doors to pursue your vision full-time.

Just don't ever fool yourself into believing that you can have so much raw talent, intelligence, strength, or any other natural gifts that you can just instantly carry these into an office, hang a sign on the door and start making money. You'll regret that you wasted so much time and energy. Don't you think there are men and women somewhere in the world who are smarter than billionaire Bill Gates? More beautiful than the most famous supermodels? With all the people on earth, there has to be! But did they take the time to develop skill? Are they computer geniuses like Bill Gates, who never went to business school to learn what he learned? Are they gorgeous women who tripped when they walked, instead of training to glide gracefully down the runway? This is the only thing that separates so many of the greatest achievers from the rest of us. If you listen to the best-known personalities, many of them will admit they always thought someone else was better. They'll tell you they always admired another person, and that person is sometimes one whom the world will never know nearly as well. Another thing you might hear them say is that they had great teachers. If you watch television shows like "A&E Biography," you'll get an idea of what kinds of people and circumstances helped shape the experiences of the world's best-known achievers. These types of documentaries are not only motivating, but educational in ways that go far beyond informing us about the lives of the people they discuss. A lot of times, it comes out that a trainer or a tutor, a personal mentor, or some other kind of teacher made the greatest impact on the outcome of this achiever's career.

We know that teachers aren't just the men and women sitting in front of the classroom, the ones who give us homework at the end of the day when we're in grade school or research assignments when we're in college. Teachers come in all forms and serve in all capacities. There's no legal restriction on our ability to learn from anyone who has wisdom to pass along. There's only the perception that certain types of learning are more valuable than other types. This sort of thinking makes it easy for us to miss some of our most important lessons. Those who pick up the subtle lessons as well as the direct instructions become candidates for the "A&E" channel.

The main thing to keep in mind is that the teaching role can also apply to you as a business owner. If it serves you well as CEO to groom a manager to interact with your staff or contractors, recognize this. We only make ourselves look better and smarter when we put smart, capable people in key positions with our companies. Your role as a mentor might be the most logical one if there appears to be a more natural fit between the person you groom to handle certain operations and those he or she encounters at work. I've hired a lot of men, mainly because civil engineering is a male-dominated field. You'll probably find yourself in the same position if you're a woman who wants to own an auto repair shop, or if you're a man who wants to open a beauty salon. Teaching an employee or business partner what you've learned about the field and how to avoid certain mistakes could be a bigger contribution than you've previously imagined. It could even wind up being the difference between your company's success and failure.

You may choose to think of yourself as the coach, building a team of star players. In fact, every president or CEO is a coach. Like me, a lot of them also choose to play an active part in the day-to-day operation of the team. This is where applying wisdom comes in: when it's time to decide just how hands-on you should be from one day to the next. Much of the decision will depend on the size of your company, especially when you're just starting out. If you've begun with a partner, hired someone in a role like administrative assistant, or created a working relationship that involves only a similarly small staff, you'll find that a lot of times you can accomplish plenty through having telephone conferences and exchanging e-mail. As your business grows, it might become obvious that your physical presence is needed for more direct supervising.

Whether it's for adding your womanpower or manpower to the hard labor, taking orders by telephone, or just signing employee time sheets at the end of the week, logical openings for you to fill will make themselves known. If your company remains home-based, increasing business demands will dictate even more clearly what kinds of strategies are necessary. Then your challenge will become more a matter of coaching the rate of your company's development and progress than a matter of coaching those you hire. On the other hand, you'll have an equally great challenge: a family to coach and household concerns to prioritize between your working hours, and, believe me, that can be just as tricky as coaching professionals. I'll share with you the tips that have helped me navigate through *that* territory in a later guideline.

Knowing what part you should play gets you off to a good start, not only because of the advantages it offers you as the leader, but because it helps to set the tone for your relationship with employees, contractors, and customers. Did you ever have a supervisor who irritated you by constantly breathing down your neck and looking over your shoulder? This kind of boss doesn't usually recognize that he or she is creating distractions from the work he or she wants done by constantly interrupting, asking questions, or criticizing before they've seen finished assignments. If you found that kind of supervisor irritating, you certainly don't want to become that kind of boss, because you'll remember how much it took away from your ability to be productive. If you decide your role will be the customer relations manager and that you'll have a partner to supervise staff, you have pretty well made certain that employees know you aren't the kind of boss who'll get in their way and then wonder why they haven't completed tasks on time. On the flip side, clients who expect to see the owner of the company every time they visit your office may be comforted because you've chosen to play a part that puts them in direct contact with the head of operations. This is a role every customer appreciates, because they can feel more confident that you will handle them with care when they see you supporting their business.

There's really no way to go wrong when you determine what part you'll play early in the game. If it takes a bit of trial and error, that's OK, but your early moves and decisions will always set the tone. Make this choice a big part of your preparation and you'll be glad you did. Confidence in your handling of this choice will increase confidence in your handling of the choices to come. Look at yourself in the mirror and simply ask the question, "What's my role?" Know that throughout history, from ancient to contemporary times, the most victorious men and women have always been those who put themselves in the right position to succeed—whether personally or professionally.

"Learn What Part You Should Play."

SEVEN POWERFUL POINTERS

1. Recognize the importance of every role that is required to run your business.

    a. Romans 12:6
    b. 1 Corinthians 12:8–10

2. Consider the importance of good recordkeeping to help keep track of growth trends and other important issues relative to your business.

    a. 1 Chronicles 16:4
    b. Ezra 6:2
    c. Isaiah 8:1–2

3. Develop your natural gifts through training.

    a. Romans 11:29
    b. 1 Corinthians 12:29–31

4. Know the value of becoming a "coach" for your company team.

    a. 2 Chronicles 10:6–7

5. Identify the "natural fit" within your staff and with your customers.

    a. 1 Corinthians 12:11–12

6. Place yourself in the position to succeed.

    a. Joshua 1:7–8

7. Teachers come to us from unexpected places, so be alert to the possibilities.

    a. Proverbs 5:13
    b. Isaiah 30:20–21
    c. Ephesians 4:11–12

ALWAYS PLAY FOR THE HOME TEAM

Remember that this is a book of strategies that have helped me in my life as a wife, mother, and entrepreneur—*not* a book of rules. Strategies are specific ideas and tactics that will help you get to the destination you desire. In this case, the destination is the place that allows you enjoyment of a healthy, happy balance between household harmony and business ownership.

From childhood we've been taught that rules are not to be broken. In the home I grew up in, there was typically *some* kind of punishment associated with disobeying the rules of the home. It is important to teach our children to be obedient to the rules within our home, and the biblical rules that have been set for us by God. Disobedient children ultimately become disobedient adults. When rules are disobeyed, chaos results. Some of us have never had problems obeying rules and some of us have always wanted to make the rules ourselves. While owning a business allows you to become a rule-maker, maintaining healthy families requires that you follow one set of rules, even as the parent. It's the rule of our Higher Authority, the "Big Boss," so to speak.

The only rules you'll read about in this book are these: Be obedient to the teaching and instruction of the Word of God and always strive to treat others in a loving, caring manner. The guidelines I suggest for you are designed to be tailored to your specific goals and visions. It's not a bad thing if you find yourself adding a detail or taking a bit away from the approaches that I recommend. These are the principles that have worked for me, but you will always have to use your best judgment in making the strategies fit, based on the structure of your family and business, stage of life you're experiencing, career field, and other specifics. Be willing to search for the resources you trust as a guide to achieve an accomplishment as major as running your own successful business and maintaining a peaceful, orderly home. We'd all like to make our own schedules, be our own bosses and make good money doing it, but the reason so many businesses fail is it's just not that easy. There is one book that I have chosen to obey that tells me how to raise and maintain a happy and healthy family. My preference of a book that provides guidelines for daily living is the Bible. Strategies should give a realistic approach in the quest to obtain success, but you have to follow the *rule* of playing for your home team.

Again, this might seem like an obvious point. You're looking out for home by creating a better business opportunity for yourself that will benefit your loved ones. The key is to recognize how far you should go at each point in the development of your business. When there's a need for sacrifice and your only choices are business and home, you should make the decision of the best way to first sacrifice business. I'm not telling you to plan on packing up and closing shop at the first sign of trouble or conflict, but be prepared to put any part of your business owner experience—whether it's the planning stage or the grand opening—on hold if necessary. Never do anything that will cause your spouse or your children to question how much they can depend on you.

Emergency situations are easy calls to make. Drop everything you're doing if the family has an urgent need. I'm stressing that you should keep a close eye on the less pressing issues that may turn out to be just as important. Don't get so caught up in a client meeting that you lose track of time and miss the dance recital. If you do good work, you'll keep that client, but your child may not forget that you broke your promise. Don't treat your spouse like a live-in babysitter. While you're putting in extra hours, your spouse may want to get a massage or go play a round of golf. It's easy to shift focus from the people we live with and interact with every day when we take on something else that excites and challenges us. It's a lot harder to correct the problems that can result when we lose that focus for too long. Poor grades and behavior issues with the children can take so much time and energy to correct that your business will wind up suffering anyway. A husband or wife who feels resentful about your work can make it impossible for you to keep pursuing your goals by refusing to support you.

I was fortunate in that I had a lot of practice playing for the home team before I ever became a wife and mom. Often events and circumstances that occur early in our lives will prepare us for the future without our knowing it. My father was an educator in Flint, Michigan, and my mother was a homemaker and nurse's aide. I was the youngest of a family of four children. We weren't what you would call *well off* financially, and that wasn't always easy, but I had a loving and stable upbringing, for which I'm thankful. Knowing what I do now, I realize that my parents had challenges I didn't even recognize as a child. Raising a family in a working-class community had its benefits, nevertheless.

Flint is primarily a blue-collar town about an hour's drive from Detroit, but not nearly as large. If you're not from Southeast Michigan, you may not even be familiar with the city at all.

When I was growing up, Flint was largely supported by the automobile manufacturing factories. Many families were supported by workers on the assembly lines and many home mortgages were paid through these salaries. Filmmaker Michael Moore's 1989 movie *Roger & Me* documented the downsizing of General Motors and its effect on the Flint workforce. Fortunately, my personal course had been pretty much established. Not that I can say I knew I would own an engineering firm, but I more or less knew I would be independent as an adult. I was already an independent thinker who took the initiative. What we used to call *taking the initiative* is now called being a "self-starter." Self-starters tend to get a lot of praise on the job, because they inspire supervisors to believe they work harder than others. It's a lot easier to appreciate the employee who proposes ideas, improvements, and changes that can help the team and the company than the person who only waits to do what he or she is told. If you haven't been a self-starter it might be harder to recognize one, but keep in mind that these types will be the best to recruit for your business when you get to the hiring stage. Even a housekeeper who finds new ways to clean floors more thoroughly and save space in storage closets will stand out from one who does the bare minimum in your office space. The self-starting process began to come naturally for me when I was still a child.

I was so young I don't remember many of the issues related to my mother's inner turmoil, but eventually I learned that she was affected by the mental illness of paranoid schizophrenia. What I do recall is that I did my part at being a little helper around the house. I took care of chores all by myself and did schoolwork without having to be reminded. I can clearly remember being a part of the family support system when I was very small and my mother wasn't noticeably present; I didn't excessively question the reason. I know that my father and older siblings were supporting the household and helping her cope with her condition at the same time, so it was a good thing that God made me the way I was.

One burden my parents needed even less than other moms and dads was children who created problems for them. So I was learning to play for the home team before I understood the concept of who the *real* home team was. I don't share all of this to brag on myself, but it's interesting to think of how our personal experiences can shape our careers. I get the feeling that if I were a spoiled child with two parents who were always healthy, I'd never have gone into business for myself. I would have been more accustomed to waiting for things to happen than *making* them happen. As it turned out for me, making things happen at home was training for the things I would later make happen in the business world. For others, it works out in just the opposite manner, but this is partly why so many families experience the problems I'd like to help you avoid.

While many of us do it, it's not fair to plan our families around our careers. Careers should be structured to accommodate families. You've probably heard people say things like, "I'm going to wait until the kids start kindergarten before I go back to work," or, "I can't retire until the children graduate from college." This may sound like sensible, responsible adult thinking, and it is. But sometimes it indicates a failure to plan ahead. Too many parents *want* to retire, but can't because they've committed to paying tuition. Too many mothers *want* to go back to work, but can't because their children are still dependent on them. We just think of these as the loving sacrifices parents will make for their sons and daughters; however, becoming an entrepreneur will provide you a chance to see into the future.

One of the greatest sacrifices a parent can make is building a professional and financial legacy to pass along to younger generations. If you carefully create and follow a business plan based on your research and preparation, you stand a better chance of working— because you want to, not because you have to. You also stand a better chance of keeping your career moving as the children grow. The plus-side of creating a successful business versus remaining employed by a company is that you can control your hours and your rate of expansion. You can foresee the necessary adjustments that may have to be made for securing the enterprise. We know that planning, when it comes to childbirth, child-care, and family issues in general, is never going to be an exact science. Despite this, it can be much more practical than we think if we link family planning with careful career strategy. This is all the more reason for you to use your years of training and on-the-job experience as testing ground before you take on the duties of CEO.

Through your training and preparation time, you should not only get as much knowledge as possible, but you should also explore as many options as your field presents. Business opportunities will reveal themselves more clearly as you immerse yourself in training. There are multiple paths to the same goal of owning a company, even when your field has been chosen. One of the worst mistakes you can make is pouring your time and money into a business that leaves you unfulfilled. You might just as well have kept your old job! Focusing on regrets that you didn't consider the best angle for approaching your goal will be a distraction that's costly in more ways than just the obvious ones.

In my journey, I graduated in 1979 from Beecher High School before leaving home to attend Michigan State University. By 1983 I had earned a degree from Michigan State in Civil and Environmental Engineering. I knew I wanted to marry and have children, but it wasn't something I was in a major hurry to do. Even though I dated, it wasn't a distraction for me in the way that it can sometimes be for a college student. Again, I think our attitudes toward responsibility from an early age prepare (or don't prepare) us for this stage. The freedom and flexibility of a campus environment can make or break a young person just starting out. Those who've had practice with self-discipline are usually better able to handle the challenge than those who relied on instruction and supervision. I gained valuable work experience while working at Sears Roebuck and Company during my high school years and through internships in my field of study while I fulfilled course requirements. It was through this early exposure to the world of engineering internships I received as a student that I obtained the sense of familiarity with the industry and its demands that I discussed in the previous principle. Getting a general sense of what I'd encounter as an engineer was a helpful orientation, though I wasn't yet qualified to perform the actual work.

A year after my undergraduate college graduation and internship experiences, in 1984, I married Michael Foster. Now the real fun would begin! It was fortunate for me that I didn't have much of a balancing act to manage, aside from my own obligations and schedule, until Mike came along. The rest of my journey would involve my husband, and eventually two sons. It was the beginning of the vision that became what my life is today. I can remember praying to God for the blessings of a husband who loved me, a family I could nurture, and a fulfilling career. I remember asking God to give me the wisdom to make decisions that would place me in a lifestyle where I would not have to worry about money. These were my simple prayers. I believed in God, but my walk with Him was less than righteous at the time. The answer to my prayers from God was for me to be obedient to His teaching and instruction in my daily life. After about four years of marriage, my husband and I made a commitment to begin living a more righteous, godly life.

I was blessed with a loving husband who had similar beliefs and desires for us, but I also wanted to make my own contributions as a wife, mother, and entrepreneur. We were beginning to build our home team. I didn't want to watch from the sidelines. Home was a place where I had always felt like I was a key player, so why should anything be different now? This was the time to lay a foundation for what my parents had prepared me to do, even as they worked to meet the challenges in their household. Successfully building a family of my own would be the kind of tribute they could appreciate. Any parent who sees a child he or she has raised do well in establishing a brand new household feels the same sense of honor. I knew it would serve as a gift to my parents and my future children if I could play a part in that blessing. But first I focused on adding the professional credentials that would later qualify me to create BBF Engineering Services. The funny thing is I never actually set out to start my own company; all I did was follow the direction from God that I was given after I prayed for those blessings. What I learned through the process is what I'm able to share with you.

I was working at Bechtel Power Corporation in Ann Arbor, Michigan, when I met Mike. The experience at Bechtel was my first full-time engineering position after graduating from Michigan State, but it still served as a sort of trial period for me. Based on my education and training, I had the choice of pursuing *structural* engineering or *general civil* engineering, and I had trouble deciding which way to go. It was early enough in my career that if I started in one direction, there wouldn't be a problem with me changing toward another. Since my undergraduate studies at Michigan State focused on structural engineering, at Bechtel I held a position as a structural engineer, but it became monotonous, so in 1985 I moved into the civil engineering area that has shaped my career. It was an important step, however, for me to explore what I might have otherwise missed if I hadn't gone to Bechtel, because I believe I would've regretted not learning what it was like to perform structural engineering as a profession. Regrets can kill your goals.

I worked as a structural engineer until I married and relocated to another city in Southeastern Michigan. At that point, I entered the road design division of the Oakland County Road Commission. This position was a good learning experience for my tenure of less than two years. Then I was recruited by the Michigan Department of Transportation (MDOT), where I found broader training and an increased salary. The Michigan Department of Transportation, like the Department of Transportation in other states, is responsible for major road and freeway construction projects, maintenance, and travel safety issues. I stayed with MDOT, eventually working my way up through the ranks to a position as a department supervisor before I left the agency and the state in 1992 after seven years. I had begun getting valuable practice at playing for the home team when it was still just Mike and me by dividing my time as a wife between work and school. By returning to the classroom, I had earned a master's degree in civil engineering at Wayne State University in 1989. I also took a crucial step by passing the exams to become certified as a licensed professional engineer.

The added education helped me qualify for what wound up being my most important position with a government transportation agency: At age thirty-two I was appointed director of Highways and Streets for the City of Atlanta under the late Mayor Maynard Jackson. During my time in Georgia, I noticed how some of the family traditions that we often neglected in our northern communities remained altogether intact in the South. Take Sunday dinner, for example. A lot of us read about how the family psychologists and other experts say there is a loss of unity in the home because so few of us even make the time to sit down at the table and have meals together anymore. While living in the South, I noticed that dinner every Sunday was still common, and not just for immediate relatives. Cousins, coworkers, and neighbors might all be invited to partake in a hearty meal at a home that wasn't their own. It might seem like a little thing, but I noticed how this tradition, along with cookouts and other similar get-togethers, added a different atmosphere to the community. Family and close friends who are expected to be at the dinner table the same way they're expected to be at their desks for work develop a sense of accountability to their families, and this accountability tends to reflect in their neighborhoods.

Consider the importance of these "little things" in your home and the value they'll add to your relationships with loved ones as you become more focused on attaining your career goals. If you've been running the kind of kitchen that works on the principle of "every man for himself," make it a priority to have sit-down meals together at least three times a week. You'll begin to notice changes in the communication among those who sit with you at the table, and you'll feel a subtle change in the energy at your home. This will be a blessing to your family!

By 1993, it was time for me to put my practice and observations to good use. We returned to Michigan where my first son, Lance, was born. Now the fun would *really* begin! I took the first steps that would help me establish a solid home and business combination and began professional consulting for engineering clients. Meanwhile, I had earned a fellowship to pursue my Doctorate Degree in Engineering at Michigan State University. As the sole proprietor of my consulting business, I had the full say of my schedule. This allowed me to be home with Lance and maintain a flexible schedule.

Consulting isn't for everybody, just like owning any form of business isn't for everybody. But it really worked in my favor. I had a professional reputation and contacts to build from, since I had worked in the industry. I could see the things I had prayed about beginning to happen. I had learned to prioritize my life such that I was able to maintain proper order: obedience to the Word of God, caring for needs of self and spouse, raising godly children, fulfilling my purpose and career, and work within the church and Kingdom of God. Family and work were forming a balance that I have managed to prioritize ever since.

Everybody has a different capacity of what they can physically and emotionally handle, depending on the nature of their livelihood and the structure of their family. There's really no exact science, but you have to gauge what you can handle by the amount of rest you're getting, the amount of income you're producing, and the amount of general stress being experienced by you and your family. One person may have three children, and another person may have only one. One person may be a single parent who gets a lot of help with babysitting from a grandparent. I was the primary caregiver for my children, especially since I did not have immediate family members who lived nearby. I was the one to nurture and take care of them, and I desired to just give *mommy time*. Not that it was always perfect, but it was comfortable for the Fosters.

By the time my second son, William, was born, it was basically a matter of following the working model I had developed. As young children, our sons asked me where I was going whenever I was leaving home without them, because they loved having all of their immediate family around. Even if I'm in the next room, they just want to know that I'm there. If you've got one child who is an infant, it might be much more difficult to handle a business than it would be if you have a twelve and thirteen-year-old. I eventually expanded the business from my home office, and my husband and I settled into roles similar to the ones you see at successful companies. As spouses, it's important that your personalities and skills complement one another. Mike was akin to the CEO in our home, because he was the primary breadwinner. His full-time work is what made our income stable when I started my consulting business. I took on the role of administrator, because I had the time and flexibility to administrate the important affairs of our household.

It's crucial to be just as committed and loyal to home duties as to the duties we're paid for on the job. Lack of commitment can cripple any family or any business, no matter how powerful. Here are some statistics from the U.S. Census Bureau about various family roles and structures that demonstrate levels of commitment to playing for the home team:

- In 2003 (the most recent year from which this data was taken), 57 million American households contained married couples.
- Regarding single parents: "Whether the single parent is divorced or never married may be an important indicator of the quality of life for children in these family groups. Children living with divorced single mothers typically have an advantage over children living with those who never married. Divorced parents are, on average, older, have more education, and have higher incomes than parents who never married."
- In 2003, 23 million married couples had children younger than age 15.
- In 2003, 6 million of 7 million mothers who stayed home from work said it was to care for the home and family, as opposed to illness, inability to find employment, or other factors; 160,000 out of 1 million dads said they stayed home for the same reason.

While there was apparently no data showing how many households produced profitable businesses, children who graduated from college, or other traditional indicators of success, the truth is suggested by the figures: playing for the home team helps earn the victory.

"Always Play for the Home Team."

SEVEN POWERFUL POINTERS

1. Careers should accommodate families, not the other way around.

    a. Proverbs 31:27

2. Create a positive legacy for your children and future generations.

    a. Deuteronomy 3:28
    b. Deuteronomy 16:20
    c. 2 Chronicles 20:10–11
    d. Psalms 25:12–14

3. Recognize and embrace the fact that God created you the way you are in order to complete the assignments you have to accomplish during your life.

    a. Genesis 1:27
    b. Isaiah 3:7
    c. Colossians 1:16

4. Recognize your spouse as the co-chairperson of your home. *You are a team!*

    a. Proverbs 12:4
    b. Proverbs 31:28
    c. 1 Corinthians 7:3

5. Dedicate yourself to having sit-down, family dinners and positive household traditions.

    a. 2 Thessalonians 2:15

6. Keep the priority God sets for the structure of your life and family.

    a. Ephesians 5:22–25
    b. Titus 2:4–5

7. Teach your children the importance of discipline and obedience.

   a. Deuteronomy 11:26–28
   b. Deuteronomy 27:10
   c. Proverbs 22:6

KNOW THE REAL COST
OF BEING THE BOSS

What image comes to your mind when you hear the word "boss?" Is it a ruthless company president who is highly arrogant, displaying a need to mistreat those who work for the company to show his "power?" A boss may run a big corporate empire and be one of the most powerful people in the city. The boss may have plenty of money, success, and a wonderful spouse, but everybody in town knows better than to cross him or her. The boss may be called names like *arrogant, unfair,* and *ruthless* because of his intimidating ways. This person doesn't *play around* when it comes to business. Whether they need to take you to court or snatch you by the collar, they're willing to prove they're tough and let you know who's in charge.

In America, this really isn't anything new. There are all sorts of wealthy celebrities and fictional characters who become our icons. There are gangster films like *The Godfather* and *The Untouchables*, where even the crime bosses are admired for their fearlessness and their skill at avoiding the long arm of the law. It's not that we necessarily appreciate the way they murder, rob, and devastate society, but we know that if the police capture them too quickly, the story's over! Bosses of all kinds become household names; people we imitate in our speech, behavior, and dress. We stop what we're doing to hear what they're saying on the radio, and then we repeat their words to our friends. We buy products that they endorse, just because they talk about how great these products are. A lot of times these leaders are so effective that they have their own successful companies and still get lucrative contracts that will help sell someone else's business or service. It might be only on the slightest, least noticeable levels, but many of us will imitate their ways and habits.

We crave to have the same images of success, even if we haven't yet achieved the success itself. We see these people on television and in newspapers getting in and out of limousines, waving to onlookers, and being interviewed about how they've done so well in their careers. We usually *don't* see them in their office meetings with employees. We *don't* see them signing pay checks. We *don't* see them negotiating the deals that bring them business. We usually *don't* see them in the most stressful moments of managing their professional lives and keeping their companies profitable and under control. Getting their hands dirty with day-to-day business responsibilities is the least glamorous work of all.

What do you think they do to get so much attention when they venture out in front of the public? How did they build their record labels, sports teams, restaurant chains, and clothing chains to the level of national or worldwide recognition? Hard work is a good guess. Long hours are pretty much a given. Finding ways to balance time between building their businesses and interacting with family members would have to have been the same challenge it will be for you.

But what about their styles of management? They had to have had some ability to motivate others to support their vision. They had to have had a way of showing others how the vision would be beneficial to the staff and contractors who were necessary in helping them achieve it. A paycheck alone is not enough for the average, healthy person to sacrifice time, energy, and rest in any position where he or she doesn't feel like his or her professional contributions are appreciated. Self-respecting employees recognize that they serve as more than just bodies at desks or on project sites. They know that they bring required skills, however vital or seemingly insignificant, that bosses need to properly run their companies. Even the least-paid staff members, whose presence at the company is barely ever thought about, know there are other jobs that require the same minor qualifications they could easily meet. Don't make the mistake of treating employees like you're doing them a favor by hiring them. They will be right to resent it, if you do. A smart employer won't project that attitude when interviewing candidates, either. If it's not obvious what a job applicant might do to help you move forward, don't waste his or her time doing the interview. Look for people who will be assets to your business, not just people who will take on a workload. A donkey can take on a load, but you wouldn't want to hire one.

It's a new concept, for most of us, to become supervisors after years of being supervised. Think about what you liked most about your previous bosses, and also think about what you liked least. Bear in mind that you will need to sell yourself and your business to any talented job-seeker, because you won't be the only boss to recognize this same talent. Serious job hunters are seriously on the hunt, and if they've shown you an impressive resume, chances are they've shown it before and may show it again. You'll have to make your opportunity look attractive if you want to recruit the best talent. There will always be times when you can't offer as much pay or as nice of a benefits package, or as many vacation days as another employer, so you'll have to find ways to positively connect with the cream of the crop. Otherwise, you may be stuck choosing from the leftovers.

Recruiting talent is tough. It's not the sort of thing you want to let your ego influence. Sure, there may be highly visible professionals who run the biggest firms in the nation and rely on their reputations to draw top talent. This works, but only for so long. Talent rises to the top, and when it's obvious that there are few places left to go in an organization without stealing the CEO's job, there's little to keep the most capable employee tethered, besides loyalty. The wealthiest, most powerful boss is not immune to a need for loyal management, staff, or even volunteers. What appeals to a job candidate when joining a high-profile leader's team won't seem as impressive after five or ten years. There has to be more than reputation and alignment with a famous company name or celebrity CEO. And there has to be more than money there.

Most of us will never know what techniques are used by the best-known heads of corporations and bosses when they're operating behind closed doors. The competition for these positions is intense, and it appears to be increasing. Fewer and fewer people are going the route that you're considering right now to try and blaze a professional trail or build reputations of their own. It is, more or less, a reflection of that same traditional mentality that tells most of us to find work, rather than to work for ourselves. The lure simply takes on an added appeal when there is the appearance of some high standing in the community attached to the position. So, it's good that this same lure helps to spark ambition. It's just a different form of ambition than what drives the future business owner. Instead of wanting to be out front leading the company, they choose to support the leader. But with the leader getting all the attention, there has got to be some skillful management at work.

There's no denying that there are real-life presidents and CEOs who rule their companies with an iron fist. Many of us know firsthand, because we've worked for them. These are the types of managers who often make up their minds about how things should work before ever consulting their assistants or staffs. They are seldom receptive to ideas or suggestions, no matter *how* the ideas and suggestions are presented. They are quick to get angry, and slow to say thanks or offer praise. The amazing thing is that bosses like this are able to keep their companies running at all. They believe that fear and intimidation are the best ways to get results from their employees, and they don't seem to consider that fear and intimidation can actually reduce the effectiveness of performance on the job.

What are normal reactions for people who become afraid? There's nervousness. Sometimes there's panic. There's distraction, sometimes to the point of feeling paralyzed. It's impossible to work well under conditions where fear is the main motivator. The major focus becomes one's ability to address the fear, not one's ability to perform with a commitment to quality. It might seem as if the two go hand-in-hand. If you're afraid of being suspended without pay, having money docked from your paycheck, losing your job, and all of the problems you and your family might experience as a result of these forms of discipline, you lose some of the mental energy that's needed to concentrate on your work. You may get it done—in fact, you'll almost *definitely* get it done just to avoid suffering the consequences—but, in one way or another, the service or product you help to provide will usually be lacking. Don't ever make the misjudgment of becoming the kind of boss who begins to think otherwise. A lower level of performance by employees is one issue, but there have even been many cases of deliberate sabotage in retaliation for cruel treatment by supervisors, who never ultimately identify the responsible party. Just be careful not to confuse being cruel with being firm. Firm leadership is not an option for the president of a company. It's just a matter of how that firmness is presented.

Throwing fits of anger is just a lot of wasted emotional energy. It won't get your point across to anyone, and it won't be the kind of behavior that your staff or customers can respect. Believe it or not, there are some bosses who will make a big show of talking down to employees in front of their clients. They don't have the basic respect for others that would prevent them from using embarrassment as discipline. Reprimands should be given in a way that shows you have a problem with a person's work, but not the person. This can be done through private meetings, or in written letters that are properly worded.

You may be disappointed or even resentful of anyone you hire who fails to show that they take your vision as seriously as you do. Be firm in dealing with the problems they create for you and your company, but don't use humiliation or any kind of abuse. You can make yourself heard without ever raising your voice, and you can be helpful in correcting problems within your staff by handling them with calmness and wisdom. Of course, there is no single, specific rule for employee management and supervision. You have to deal with individual staff members and contractors according to who they are and what their shortcomings may be. This is the same approach that we should apply as parents. We should love our children the same, but we may need to chastise them differently. Never has there been a family that had any two children who behaved, or misbehaved, in exactly the same ways. Some kids are shy by nature and tend to stay out of trouble as a result. Others are outgoing and adventurous, so they may find themselves getting into a bit more mischief. In any case, none of our sons or daughters is perfect, no matter how much we'd like to believe they are. As parents we have to determine the ways to address their individual behavior flaws. If a daughter doesn't finish her homework on time, it might be wise to restrict her television-watching hours. Her brother might not watch much television, but he might neglect his homework by putting too much effort into raking leaves and mowing grass in the neighborhood for extra cash. Limiting his business endeavors to weekends would be a more appropriate correction. The objective is to get the best possible performance out of the children in their academics. Similarly, the goal in your company is to get the best possible performance out of your team. When everyone is equally motivated to succeed, the results will show in every area of your business.

A harmonious work environment helps reduce staff turnover. Reduced staff turnover, in turn, reduces the work of recruiting, interviewing, and hiring to refill vacant positions. This will come with the territory that you face as the president of your company. It will be necessary in the beginning when you put a staff into place, and it's altogether unlikely that you'll keep *all* of your original employees if you create a long-lasting and successful business, which should be your goal. It's no big accomplishment to retain a staff if you're only in business for six months to a year. For one thing, most people prefer not to have to change jobs so quickly. The majority of job seekers would like to stay in a stable position for awhile, after going through the effort of searching for employment. Depending on the time and level of work they've spent looking for a new position, it may well be that a short stay at a company feels like a waste. The hunt can feel, for some, like the *job before the job*. As time goes on, however, it's inevitable that you'll have employees who move on. They may have children and want to stay home to raise them. Their relatives may become ill and need assistance that requires great personal sacrifices from your employees. They may simply outgrow the work they've been performing for your company and want to move on to new challenges—just as you did. In some cases, you can control this variable. In others, you cannot.

An employee who respects you as his or her boss will often let you know that the assignments and duties you've given him are no longer challenging. He or she may come right out and say that they want advancement or the opportunity to experience new aspects of the profession for which you've hired them. This should indicate to you that you've successfully connected with the employee. It means that he or she feels you've been fair, and it's a sign of faith that you will show fairness and consideration of the concerns that have been expressed to you. If this is a valuable employee, you'll be glad this person approached you. The alternative may have been that you looked on your desk one day and found a letter of resignation because your team member decided to look for opportunities elsewhere. The wise thing for you to do would be to add responsibilities that the employee can capably handle.

It may require that you give him or her some additional training, such as accompanying you to meetings—or possibly creating a new job based on the interests shared by the employee. If a pay increase has been requested, obviously you will have to make another judgment call, based on your budget. The benefits of keeping top performers on your staff will always outweigh the drawbacks. Recruiting and rehiring for positions takes time away from your day–to–day operation of the business. But life affects us all in both positive and negative ways, so at one point or another you should expect to replace team members due to the individual, personal, and professional circumstances they're experiencing. Nevertheless, the temptation to leave a job is always lessened when a comfortable and respectful atmosphere that acknowledges the value of team members has been created.

Is the aggressive, self-centered supervisor model the way you can accomplish this? Maybe so, if you think you can create a respectful work environment by being the most aggressive force on your team.

The key, in a nutshell, to creating successful businesses is to get your partners, staff, volunteers, customers, and anyone else involved to *buy into your vision*. Money alone won't be enough to help you achieve this. Salaries are expected and required by people as compensation for their time, knowledge, and effort. Getting the best performance, the most creative ideas, the most valuable feedback, the commitment to quality, the loyalty of your team—these are all the added aspects you should be seeking as a president and CEO. The ability to bring out the greatest contributions from your employees is what will separate you from your competition. When you use moral, ethical, and godly principles as the umbrella over all you do, it guides everything else. If you wouldn't cheat your neighbor whom you've lived next door to for twenty years, and whose grandchildren have played with your grandchildren, you're less likely to cheat an employee who has a picture of his grandchildren on his desk.

You can't expect commitment and dedication, or even enthusiasm, from employees who don't sense that you care about their well-being. If they sense that your concern extends beyond the time spent on your payroll, they are more likely to return the same level of interest and consideration to their work on your behalf. I interviewed a lady for a position with my company, and she told me that she had a good job in Texas, but she was moving back to Michigan because her mother was sick. That showed good character and the kind of devotion that I want, and other employers would want, to represent the interests of their company. Sacrifices come in various ways. There's nothing wrong with making sacrifices, but we have to place ourselves in positions where we don't sacrifice more than we can afford.

Within the last three or four years of being my own boss I began feeling like I needed a mentor, but I knew I had to be very careful in choosing one. Some people who *could* have been good business mentors to me had passed away. I didn't want to reach out to ask for mentorship, just to say that I had a mentor with a person I didn't know well or feel comfortable with. My Dad had always been that trusted person to me, and he'd passed away in April, 2002. It's one thing to get professional mentorship from people who can help you learn the field you're entering; however, it's different when you look at confiding in someone about the problems and challenges of starting and running your own business. I know of people who've had mentors who were genuinely helpful and interested in their wellbeing—but who weren't so pleased when the time came for them to move into their own business ownership and become potential competitors with their mentors.

A mentor may only be comfortable until the time when his or her student is rising to the skill level of the teacher. This doesn't mean they aren't good people, but because they are human, it may mean they have insecurities that may take even *them* by surprise if they were to recognize them. Ultimately we all have to accept the responsibilities of leadership for our company teams. Select a mentor who is confident in his own accomplishments and can genuinely encourage you throughout the tribulations and triumphs of your journey.

Gaining great contributions from your team will result in a reputation that attracts customers to your vision. It will put you in the same league of leadership as bosses like Oprah Winfrey. Having vision is what transformed her from the professional status of an unknown nineteen-year-old television broadcaster to one of the most recognized faces in the entire world. *Translating her vision* is what moved her from the position of supervising the staff of a television show that carried her name to overseeing operations of several different companies that carry it. Depending on the nature of your work, you may or may not ever achieve the same type of name recognition and visibility for your business enterprise that Oprah has. Remember, this example of success is not meant to get you thinking you should hold yourself to anyone else's standard of achievement. For example, a person who is married with children should not compare their career and business progress with a person who is single, without children, and vice versa. The degree of career and business focus, in addition to raising children and providing emotional support to a household, will vary for each family situation.

Who knows what may have become of this great woman's career if she had started it as a mother of four? There's no reason to say she couldn't have accomplished just as much as she did while single and childless, but it's reasonable to believe that she may have accomplished it over a longer period of time. And would she have accomplished it in a way that left her family feeling neglected, as if they were less important than her career as a media celebrity? Would her husband have felt like he was an insignificant partner in their marriage? Would the children have felt emotionally distant from their mom? These are all vital questions as you consider what you yourself want to achieve.

If you can build a business by gaining the support of others in pursuing your vision and still answer in the negative to similar questions about your family once your company is doing well, you've gained it all. In fact, you've outdone many of the most powerful CEOs in the world, because most of these leaders can never quite match the level of achievement in their business endeavors when they put family accomplishments next to them. They are almost always unequally driven to match their professional passions with their personal concerns. This is why it is so important to implement the priority God has ordained for our lives.

This is where being the boss becomes a more subtle and less formal task. There are parallels between supervising your business vision and supervising the vision you have for your home. You should consider yourself to be in the same position of authority over the operations of your household as you are over your business concerns. Nonetheless, you can't hire and fire your family members! It does no good for you to think about professional qualifications and what they bring to the talent pool—because they're linked with you for the rest of your life. No one will ask you about career advancement or opportunities that require you to think about whether you are up to specific professional tasks. So the rules of success in the family will become different—much different in some respects.

On the other hand, the guideline for knowing the cost of being the boss will still apply. You'll still want to make your organization—the family team—seem appealing. You'll still want your loved ones to feel a sense of loyalty and to give their best to you and to each other. If you were raised the way I was raised, I understand. I was taught that children respect adults and do what they're asked to do. This is the natural order of all families. It doesn't show love or support for our sons and daughters to allow them to have freedoms they aren't mature enough to use wisely. It doesn't do the household any good to allow the children's wishes to dictate our schedules, our priorities, or our day-to-day activities and operations. Indulging them is one thing, but giving them too much *control* is a recipe for disaster.

If we're not careful in balancing our business focus with our home focus, we can hand over control to our children without even realizing it. Poor supervision in the home can have similar results to poor supervision within the company: We lose touch with the quality of our products and services. If we give our children control, they become the forces behind the quality of their own behavior and performance in public and private.

If we wouldn't let this happen in the businesses we've invested money and time to build, it's that much more important that we maintain *quality control* in the lives and behavior of our precious loved ones. So, I'm not arguing that the team approach be adapted in your home at the expense of keeping things in their proper perspective.

Children should still be treated like children. Where discipline, guidance, and correction are required, they should never be sacrificed. That would be like ignoring a complaint from one of your biggest clients about one of your staff members. Nevertheless, there's nothing wrong with persuading family members to buy into your vision for the family. Showing them how smoothly things can run, how much time you can spend together, or how much fun you can enjoy will always be more effective in getting them to contribute their best than telling them to do things, "Because I said so." Remember, you don't pay your family members, so giving orders has limited power. It's not because they won't follow your instructions, but because they won't learn anything from instructions they don't understand. They'll just know they had to do something. It's important to make the connection between the member of the family team and the impact of the member's behavior on the family.

For instance, suppose there is an issue involving a child who constantly runs behind schedule. You've established a routine. Bedtime is set, and so is the time for everyone to get up in the morning. You're a regular *Super Parent*. You do it all. You make breakfast in the morning. You prepare lunch for the children to take to school, and you personally drive them to class every morning before that first bell rings. All of this takes place before you even begin your action-packed days as the CEO of your own business. Maybe you've got some support from a husband or wife who helps you manage all of this, but maybe you're divorced and handling it alone. Whatever the case, it's important to you that things go according to plan—because it's harder on you when they don't. How are you going to ensure this?

No parent prefers to be in the position of making up a strategy after work and school days are already in motion. But, for some reason, your nine-year-old son is never at the breakfast table to eat his fruit and oatmeal while it's still warm. He's brushing his teeth in pajamas when he should be putting on his socks and shoes. By the time you and your daughter are ready to head out the door, he's just getting himself to the kitchen. Now you've got to go through the extra trouble of putting his breakfast into a portable container or finding him something else he can eat in the car without making a mess!

You may be thinking that the quickest way to fix this problem is to let him go hungry until lunchtime. Depending on the situation and the other alternatives you may have tried, this may be a last resort but, in the end, if you do this, your son won't understand anything except that when he moves too slowly he doesn't get his breakfast. The more effective move, the one that will create a lasting impact, will be the one that helps your son to see how his tardiness causes a problem outside of *his* particular concern. Explain to him that you care about him very much, and this is why you want to make certain he doesn't go to school hungry in the morning. Tell him that it takes work in the morning for you to prepare his breakfast and that the food you buy gets wasted when he isn't dressed and ready in time to eat it. Maybe you could also point out how unfair it is that his sister has to sit around, uncomfortably, with her coat on while she waits for him to get prepared for class. The biggest concern is that they will both be late to school and this may cause you to be late for meetings or other work responsibilities. Explain that being the boss of your company requires you to set the best example of how your staff should handle their work.

The shortcut to the message in all of this? Your son learns how his lateness affects the way that everybody in the household (and company) starts the day. It's not just a matter of whether he gets to eat breakfast in the morning. His running late makes *everyone* feel a little more stressed and forces you to have to work harder than necessary. Now he should understand that as a member of the team, he'll have to focus on moving quickly and avoiding distractions that might otherwise prevent him from doing his part to help with the team effort.

It's easy enough to apply this form of motivation to other situations, too. Getting our children to do their household chores is a common enough challenge. If they receive an allowance or other monetary compensation, it's not unreasonable to dock their pay for poor performance, just like a supervisor would in a normal job. Yet, again, we need to reinforce understanding that everybody in the home should carry his or her own weight, and when one person fails to do this, someone else is affected. It's not necessary to always be so formal in running your home the same way you run your business. In fact, it's not good to make this your standard practice. After all, home should feel like home, not like a corporation, right? Still, you'll be amazed how often what works in business will also work at home. There are even times when you'll find that what works at home will work in business.

The art of negotiation and the skill of effective communicating can help us in nearly every aspect of our personal and professional lives. When we gain strength in one area, we can carry it over to others and use it to our advantage. So, the *real* cost of becoming the boss has nothing to do with payroll. It's discovering how to use the gifts and skills that we develop to get the best possible results. There are times when we can motivate our team members in the most subtle of ways. It doesn't have to be a matter of reminding employees who signs their paychecks or telling family members who pays the bills. Neither does it have to involve giving raises, promotions, or expensive personal gifts and rewards. These things should be done out of generosity and respect for our staffs, or out of love and appreciation for our families. They shouldn't be the methods we use in persuading them to do their best and contribute their all, because we want them to do this automatically.

It shouldn't take a bribe to get your team members to give 100 percent. On the contrary, the best leaders find ways to use motivation as a means of helping others see the potential in themselves. Making them feel valuable is a part of that, but getting them to make valuable contributions is the next step. There's no complex formula involved. And there's no sure way to determine if what motivates one person will motivate someone else.

There are employees who are extremely competitive. You will often find this kind of competition in sales fields that involve commissions or incentive pay that allows employees to earn unlimited salaries based on the amount they sell. Account executives often work on a commission basis. Real estate agents typically earn a percentage of the cost of a home they sell to a buyer. There are positions with places like travel agencies that offer opportunity for their representatives to earn a portion of the cost associated with a tour package they sell to a vacationer. New car dealerships often work the same way. Any number of career fields offer salaries that are based mainly on how much or how little hustling of customers the employee is willing to do to make his income.

These sales-related positions aren't for everyone, because they can be a tough way to earn a living. The way you work dictates the way you eat and the way your family eats. It's not unheard of that commission jobs may come without health benefits or sick pay. These positions tend to attract the most *driven* types of professional men and women. They like knowing that their earning potential is not limited, and they enjoy the sense of independence that comes from making and closing deals with clients, even if they make these transactions as representatives of other businesses or firms. The range of professional fields and companies that work out this kind of arrangement, however, is limited.

In engineering, commission-based salaries wouldn't work well for the simple reason that it's a more task-oriented industry. My company, BBF Engineering Services, receives contracts that call for performance by the people I hire, as opposed to contracts that offer service from a third party. The nature of sales is that the salesperson fulfills his or her biggest obligations to you once they've gotten your financial commitment. The product or service is made available through the company the salesperson represents. So, the only real pressure a representative experiences is making the sale. But only businesses and companies that can afford to provide commission as a sales incentive will find this useful as a motivation technique. Not only is the money a strong incentive, but holding titles like "top-seller" tends to appeal to professionals in fields that recognize this kind of achievement. If you start a business that doesn't involve sales commissions, you'll need a few other tricks of the trade to keep your team's spirit up—motivated for every challenge.

I'll share with you a few simple suggestions from business leaders, along with some techniques that have worked well for me. *Advance praise* is a great way to start getting positive responses from your team. When you're just starting your company and still feeling your way through the process of it all, you'll need the full compliment of your support crew. It may be too soon for you to realistically tell who's the brightest, the most creative, the most aggressive, or the best asset, but start right away saying positive things. No later than the end of your first week in business, you can give individual praise to team members—always in private, where you can give them your full attention—for the work they're doing. Don't just say it. *Mean it.*

You won't know early in the process of developing your organization what impact any of these people will eventually have on its success, but offer sincere words of appreciation for the fact that this individual is supporting your vision. You can state this in a variety of ways, which won't necessarily be specific. You can tell your receptionist something simple, like, "I wanted you to know that I like how pleasantly you answer the phone. Have a good weekend." Now if your receptionist doesn't automatically know that pleasantness is a requirement for answering phone calls to the company, you should have never hired that receptionist, but it will be a nice surprise to hear you acknowledge it, especially so early on. He or she will appreciate that you're a boss who notices positive things, one who doesn't come across as the type who can't wait to issue a write-up. Furthermore, since you will have already set the bar high, your new receptionist will be more eager to show you what else he or she can do.

The same technique can apply to any position. Take, for example, a technician who handles the items customers bring into your appliance repair shop. By the end of his first week on the job he may appear to have only average skills; nothing more and nothing less than what he represented to you on his resume. You could tell him something like, "I really appreciate how clean you leave your work area at the end of each day. It makes it easier to see how much room we've got for the next day's orders." See how easy that is?

Remember your first weeks at a brand new job and how eager you were to impress the supervisor? You wanted to back up that positive spin you put on yourself during your job interview. All new employees experience that initial willingness to please and show themselves worthy. Using the *advance praise* technique gives them a little bit of what they're looking for right away and will, hopefully, give you more of what you're looking for down the line. The only requirement is that you be consistent.

You can't use advance praise by starting off as the kind of boss who never gives compliments and never comments on work performance unless there's something negative to be said. But you also can't start off by praising your team members for the relatively small things they do and then overlook it when they start working harder and making bigger contributions. Don't forget that this is what you were motivating them to do in the first place. You shouldn't let another three months go by after giving those first compliments. If you've put the right team in place and you use the advance praise method properly, you will notice that, as time goes on, you don't have to look as hard for positive things to say.

I'm sure you've heard about other common practices companies use to boost morale and motivate employees. One of the more popular corporate efforts is the *staff retreat*. These events take place for various lengths of time, ranging from about half-a-day to overnight stays. Often they will involve in-service activities, workshops that cater to the specific, overall goals of the business. Other retreats offer casual, relaxed, environments that move the focus of participants away from job-oriented discussion and exercises, instead placing emphasis on socialization and acquaintanceship between coworkers. There are advantages to either approach, especially when retreats are organized properly.

The formal, in-service assignments usually provide instruction and information that staff members can take back to the office. They also offer opportunities for the staff to discuss the problems and challenges they are facing, then have a facilitator address their concerns. This sort of motivational forum hopes to produce an enthusiastic group of participants who can't wait to get back to work and put the new ideas and fresh approaches they've learned into action. It takes for granted that they are professionals who want to improve and increase their performance level at work. Retreats of this nature tend to be most commonly used in white-collar organizations that are larger in structure and have more challenging variables and aspects to achieving team goals. If you start a concrete finishing company, retreats would more than likely be a waste of time for you and your contractors. What other "perks" might motivate these teams more fittingly? A contest with monetary bonuses for the winning coworker team?

There are similar opportunities that allow you, the boss, to interact with your team members in a way that removes work as the primary focus. A retreat that features group activities that are fun, but structured around creating a sense of unity and teambuilding, can accomplish as much as or more than one that presents an agenda centered around the actual job. Letting your employees see one another (and letting them see you) as ordinary people is a way to help them see other interests you may have in common. When they can discuss birthdays, anniversaries, children, neighborhood concerns, hobbies, favorite restaurants, the church they attend, or any general subjects that may connect them more closely in their private thoughts and behaviors, it lets coworkers build a better working foundation. It can strengthen their devotion and loyalty to one another…and to you.

Think about what it did for your relationship with a coworker when you found out that he or she had a son or daughter who played in the same little league as your child, or a husband or wife who was a member of the same health club as yours. You probably bonded with that person, at least a little bit more closely, on the personal level. They were no longer just the guy who sat in the cubicle at the end of the hallway. They became someone you shared a few more pleasant words with now and then, and maybe looked forward to having lunch with now and then. All of this bonding can be valuable to you as a boss because it promotes dedication to the company, even if only in an indirect way. This is why you find businesses that sponsor their own softball and bowling teams: There is strength in numbers, but only when the numbers join together for mutual gain and benefit. If the benefit is having fun and *winning together* outside of work, the desire to support one another and win together on the job tends to go along with it.

On smaller levels, special events such as company picnics and office parties can help to fulfill a similar purpose to that of the retreat or extracurricular activity. But these types of things tend to be viewed more as rewards than motivators for increased professional achievement. It's not as if the Christmas get-together you host will put your staff in the mind of work. More than likely, it will put them more in the mind of finishing their gift-shopping lists, picking up items for the holiday dinner, and enjoying time *away* from the company.

You've performed some kind of miracle if you can motivate employees to the point that they never have anything except work on their minds. But you don't want robots running your company, either. They rust! The goal and the challenge you face in becoming a successful CEO is influencing others to give all they've got when they're in your service, not to take over their lives. You want to have it all, which includes a happy home experience, and you should want this for your team members, too.

A sure way to create resentment within your staff is to show them double standards. If you insist that they put in extra hours, be certain to let them see you doing the same thing every now and then. It would probably anger you to see your boss changing into casual clothes and ducking out early if he or she were the type that yells when you come back five minutes late from lunch. Put yourself in the place of everyone you hire. You can't expect a degree of commitment from others that you don't require of yourself. A common trait of the best-known and most successful CEOs is that they won't let anyone else outwork them. It doesn't matter that they're the bosses and it shouldn't matter that you are, either. My work week is typically longer than forty hours, even though I'm the president. This is a reflection of both the fact that I'm passionate about my career and the fact that I'm still driven to build my company.

Another cost of being the boss is that you stay self-motivated. If you've found a vision partner, he or she should always be there for backup, but the bulk of the weight falls on *your* shoulders. When you let your employees and contractors see you working hard, you better position yourself as a leader. You can tell them to go home sometimes and let them know you're willing to be the last person out of the building. They will appreciate your awareness that they have lives away from work and, at the same time, they will observe your dedication.

Other traditional motivators that have been used as employee incentives are: bonus pay, scheduling preferences, extra hours off, and even plain, old staff meetings. Employees like to feel like their opinions matter. Remember to be innovative in everything you do, and stay flexible. What you learn at every stage in the process of developing your business should be used as wisdom to be applied at later stages. You may begin by giving merit bonuses to your top performers and later recognize, as you get to know them, that your employees have their own family and personal commitments. Perhaps they'll be even more grateful and work harder for you if they know they can earn the chance to leave early on Fridays after completing all of the week's assignments.

This is your dream and you have to make it real, based on the two primary components: resources and ideas. Ideas will come to you as you continue to study, pray, and meditate, but also as you observe the business and staff in progress. Don't look at failure as an option. Look at failure as something that only happens when you run out of ideas. Don't be discouraged if not every idea turns out to be the best one. You won't know how to improve if you always get it right the first time. There is a reason the biggest organizations undergo corporate restructuring, mergers, and the other types of transformations that make headlines on the business pages. *You know what?* Someone had an idea. All it means is that executives spoke to one another and considered ways that they could improve the overall operations. Obviously they didn't just wake up in the morning and decide they'd like to shake things up. They gave matters a good deal of consideration, and probably looked over a lot of company trends and market data. Conclusions from their analysis and observation would have to suggest that their ideas would lead to greater profits for the company, and possibly additional benefits, including pay increases to the employees, expansion of the customer base, or an overall increased presence among the competition, if they risked making changes. And be certain of this: all change involves risk!

No major business overhaul is ever expected to do anything besides put the business in a better position than it was in prior to the restructuring. It's still a hit-or-miss attempt, but the *hit* has to have a much better chance, or it's not worth the time, energy, and effort. The goals of any boss—in any business, in any industry—whether the company exists in its initial form, or after it has been overhauled for strategic purposes, should be to get all team members to a certain, optimal level of performance and capability for growth.

There should never be a system for evaluating our loved ones at home, even when we find ourselves effectively using some of the same motivational techniques we use with employees. We still have to be careful to create a sense of separateness from work for the emotional benefit of our families. Encouragement in the form of words, hugs, and kisses are a lot more useful in the home than at formal performance assessments. Remember, if you have a spouse, it's probably not a good idea to assess your husband or wife, anyway. In the home structure, you should consider him or her your partner in everything related to day-to-day affairs. There should be no management or supervision of the adult that helps you support your home in the same way you may manage or supervise the children. It might be more appropriate to imagine your spouse and yourself as co-chairmen of a company board, one on which you *both* have voting powers and decision-making ability.

Be willing to compromise because your mate will, hopefully, have goals and dreams worth pursuing, just like you do. Don't be ready for a divorce because your spouse isn't always willing to drop everything and support *your* business effort, or because he or she doesn't see every household matter the same way you do. You *can* help strengthen support for your vision by bringing family members to the office and work site or showing them projects you've finished and photos of places you've traveled to for business. With younger children, you can even pay them up to a certain amount to do minor work at your company, gaining a tax write-off expense. By using inspiring and creative leadership, you can honor others' needs and goals and get the best out of everyone who travels with you on your professional and personal journeys.

"Know the Real Cost of Being the Boss."

SEVEN POWERFUL POINTERS

1. Remember what you liked most and least about your previous bosses.

   a. Psalms 26:4–5

2. There are parallels between the ways you manage your business and how you manage your home.

   a. 1 Timothy 3:2-4
   b. 1 Timothy 3:7

3. What motivates one person may not motivate the next.

   a. Psalms 25:5
   b. Psalms 25:9–10

4. Good leaders acknowledge when they need motivation, and they determine the best ways to motivate themselves.

   a. Romans 12:2–3

5. View the life of other bosses as a positive or negative model, not a standard.

   a. Psalms 5:8

6. Careful planning won't always prevent the occasional bad call.

   a. Psalms 25:19–21

7. The most effective bosses possess compassion, integrity, good character, and strong leadership skills.

   a. Galatians 5:22–23
   b. Ephesians 5:9

MAKE ROOM FOR CUDDLE TIME

M ommy, I don't wanna grow up," my youngest son announced. My son was sharing a few of his thoughts about the future. It was an unexpected conversation.

"No," he explained, "I just wanna stay here with you guys." There wasn't a whole lot of analysis needed to explain his statement. He was actually giving his parents a compliment. In his own way he was telling us how comfortable we'd made his home life and his childhood. It was such a comfortable place for him that he couldn't ever see himself leaving it. I feel good every time I remember that talk. Like every child who grows up, when the time comes he will be ready to leave home and create a life for himself, but I'm proud that I was able to balance my love for family and passion for work in such a way that he will take the strength of a stable and pleasant upbringing with him.

My sons have always appreciated what has become known in our household as "cuddle time." Parents should remember that it doesn't always take a trip to the arcade or the movies to make children feel like they're special to us. For my sons, *cuddle time* has always had its own way of meeting this need. What is cuddle time? It pretty much consists of one-on-one attention between a mom or dad and their child. As the word "cuddle" suggests, it usually includes an appropriate form of physical affection, but it often depends on the mood of the person needing it.

When my son says, in his endearing, low voice, "Can I have some cuddle time," I know it might mean that he's tired from doing homework and he wants a backrub. On other occasions, cuddle time might just mean that I sit on the edge of the bed with one of the boys talking with him and rubbing his back until he falls asleep. The point of cuddle time is to spend it with each child individually and let him know that he is just as important as anything else I've had to do during the course of the day. It lets them see that my time with them is a priority. No matter how long I've been gone during the day, or what number of phone calls they've heard me making in the car while taking them from school to karate class, they see that I'm not too busy for them. There's no such thing as *always* when you're a business owner, where flexibility to the customer is frequently demanded. So you shouldn't expect to say that you'll *always* have your own version of cuddle time with your children in the evening at eight-o-clock. You'll just set them up for disappointment. The key is to make certain that you don't neglect that individual effort to show them attention. Once again, prioritization and balance are the key principles to having it all.

The opposite of *balanced* is unstable. Think about an unstable bridge as if you were walking across it and compare this image with the way you bridge your time between work and family. Which end of the bridge do you need to strengthen? Which end will be in danger of becoming weak if you don't add some stability to it? These are the kinds of questions engineers like me consider when examining the real infrastructure of bridges made of concrete and steel. Do everything you can to prevent that mental bridge between your loved ones and career from collapsing because one side isn't being properly secured.

Cuddle time is different than a hug in passing or a kiss as you drop the children off for school. But it still doesn't take very long—and it's pretty easy to fit in with the rest of your home and work obligations. It's much simpler than planning a birthday party or some of the other things you'll probably want to do for your children now and then. As they become older, they'll likely want more of their own space and privacy, which is natural, so you'll have to make the appropriate adjustments. Cuddling in bed might not be so comfortable or appropriate between a mom and her 17-year-old who's growing a mustache! So, another suggestion that can be incorporated with cuddle time and also used to replace it later on, as your children mature, is what we call "family time." It's also a pretty simple and stress-free concept and you've probably done it yourself, at some point, with your loved ones. It's not limited to one-on-one interaction, and you can understand it just by its name. The main point, once more, is to incorporate it into your days on a regular basis. At my home, it's divided into *discussion time* and *recreation time*.

Family discussion time can mean anything from sitting around the dinner table, sharing what our week was like, to hearing one of us express a hurtful experience that needs to be addressed. Sometimes we'll talk about the Word of God, or new things we learned at work or in school. Family recreation time, on the other hand, can be anything from taking a walk together to watching a movie or playing Monopoly®.

It serves as a reminder for us that we aren't just people who live, eat, and sleep at the same address, but people who can enjoy each other's company. It works at home in much the same way that social functions can strengthen the sense of team unity at an office or business. Don't assume that just because your son, daughter, or even your spouse, has outside interests and friends to enjoy leisure time with, that there is no interest on their part in sharing these social experiences with you. We try to have family discussion time, family recreation time, or both at least once a week. Cuddle time is more on an as-needed basis.

You'll see how easy it is to get into busy routines as your company grows and you get into a rhythm of working hard to fulfill your vision. That's the rate of progress that you control, however. With a spouse and children in the picture, their rate of progress will be considerably different, depending on the stages and commitments associated with their lives. These days, we've got date books, Palm Pilots®, BlackBerrys® and, for those business owners who invest in them, personal secretaries to help manage schedules. Well, the next several pages give you a model that I suggest you use in learning how to balance the time you spend building your business between family time and the time you put aside to care for yourself. Use it as a worksheet that will provide you with an early look at the areas where you need to cut back, add on, or readjust to create the schedule that will allow you to have it all in your career and family. It's meant for you to begin using once your company is up and running.

My goal is to keep a schedule that allows a minimum of two hours of non-committed time between the hours of four P.M. and eleven P.M. each evening, including weekends. This time should be available for use as "relax time" to settle your body and mind. Copy and reuse the model for yourself to document home and work commitments until you reach the point where you can literally see the progress you've made and where you may still need improvement. Prioritization and balance are the goals. By using the seven guidelines, I know you can achieve them.

	Monday	Tuesday	Wednesday	Thursday	Friday	Saturday	Sunday
12-1 A.M.							
1-2 A.M.							
2-3 A.M.							
3-4 A.M.							
4-5 A.M.							
5-6 A.M.							
6-7 A.M.							
7-8 A.M.							
8-9 A.M.							
9-10 A.M.							
10-11 A.M.							
11-12 A.M.							
12-1 P.M.							
1-2 P.M.							
2-3 P.M.							
3-4 P.M.							
4-5 P.M.							
5-6 P.M.							
6-7 P.M.							
7-8 P.M.							
8-9 P.M.							
9-10 P.M.							
10-11 P.M.							
11-12 P.M.							

MAKE ROOM FOR CUDDLE TIME

	Monday	Tuesday	Wednesday	Thursday	Friday	Saturday	Sunday
12-1 A.M.							
1-2 A.M.							
2-3 A.M.							
3-4 A.M.							
4-5 A.M.							
5-6 A.M.							
6-7 A.M.							
7-8 A.M.							
8-9 A.M.							
9-10 A.M.							
10-11 A.M.							
11-12 A.M.							
12-1 P.M.							
1-2 P.M.							
2-3 P.M.							
3-4 P.M.							
4-5 P.M.							
5-6 P.M.							
6-7 P.M.							
7-8 P.M.							
8-9 P.M.							
9-10 P.M.							
10-11 P.M.							
11-12 P.M.							

	Monday	Tuesday	Wednesday	Thursday	Friday	Saturday	Sunday
12-1 A.M.							
1-2 A.M.							
2-3 A.M.							
3-4 A.M.							
4-5 A.M.							
5-6 A.M.							
6-7 A.M.							
7-8 A.M.							
8-9 A.M.							
9-10 A.M.							
10-11 A.M.							
11-12 A.M.							
12-1 P.M.							
1-2 P.M.							
2-3 P.M.							
3-4 P.M.							
4-5 P.M.							
5-6 P.M.							
6-7 P.M.							
7-8 P.M.							
8-9 P.M.							
9-10 P.M.							
10-11 P.M.							
11-12 P.M.							

MAKE ROOM FOR CUDDLE TIME

	Monday	Tuesday	Wednesday	Thursday	Friday	Saturday	Sunday
12-1 A.M.							
1-2 A.M.							
2-3 A.M.							
3-4 A.M.							
4-5 A.M.							
5-6 A.M.							
6-7 A.M.							
7-8 A.M.							
8-9 A.M.							
9-10 A.M.							
10-11 A.M.							
11-12 A.M.							
12-1 P.M.							
1-2 P.M.							
2-3 P.M.							
3-4 P.M.							
4-5 P.M.							
5-6 P.M.							
6-7 P.M.							
7-8 P.M.							
8-9 P.M.							
9-10 P.M.							
10-11 P.M.							
11-12 P.M.							

	Monday	Tuesday	Wednesday	Thursday	Friday	Saturday	Sunday
12-1 A.M.							
1-2 A.M.							
2-3 A.M.							
3-4 A.M.							
4-5 A.M.							
5-6 A.M.							
6-7 A.M.							
7-8 A.M.							
8-9 A.M.							
9-10 A.M.							
10-11 A.M.							
11-12 A.M.							
12-1 P.M.							
1-2 P.M.							
2-3 P.M.							
3-4 P.M.							
4-5 P.M.							
5-6 P.M.							
6-7 P.M.							
7-8 P.M.							
8-9 P.M.							
9-10 P.M.							
10-11 P.M.							
11-12 P.M.							

MAKE ROOM FOR CUDDLE TIME

	Monday	Tuesday	Wednesday	Thursday	Friday	Saturday	Sunday
12-1 A.M.							
1-2 A.M.							
2-3 A.M.							
3-4 A.M.							
4-5 A.M.							
5-6 A.M.							
6-7 A.M.							
7-8 A.M.							
8-9 A.M.							
9-10 A.M.							
10-11 A.M.							
11-12 A.M.							
12-1 P.M.							
1-2 P.M.							
2-3 P.M.							
3-4 P.M.							
4-5 P.M.							
5-6 P.M.							
6-7 P.M.							
7-8 P.M.							
8-9 P.M.							
9-10 P.M.							
10-11 P.M.							
11-12 P.M.							

	Monday	Tuesday	Wednesday	Thursday	Friday	Saturday	Sunday
12-1 A.M.							
1-2 A.M.							
2-3 A.M.							
3-4 A.M.							
4-5 A.M.							
5-6 A.M.							
6-7 A.M.							
7-8 A.M.							
8-9 A.M.							
9-10 A.M.							
10-11 A.M.							
11-12 A.M.							
12-1 P.M.							
1-2 P.M.							
2-3 P.M.							
3-4 P.M.							
4-5 P.M.							
5-6 P.M.							
6-7 P.M.							
7-8 P.M.							
8-9 P.M.							
9-10 P.M.							
10-11 P.M.							
11-12 P.M.							

MAKE ROOM FOR CUDDLE TIME

	Monday	Tuesday	Wednesday	Thursday	Friday	Saturday	Sunday
12-1 A.M.							
1-2 A.M.							
2-3 A.M.							
3-4 A.M.							
4-5 A.M.							
5-6 A.M.							
6-7 A.M.							
7-8 A.M.							
8-9 A.M.							
9-10 A.M.							
10-11 A.M.							
11-12 A.M.							
12-1 P.M.							
1-2 P.M.							
2-3 P.M.							
3-4 P.M.							
4-5 P.M.							
5-6 P.M.							
6-7 P.M.							
7-8 P.M.							
8-9 P.M.							
9-10 P.M.							
10-11 P.M.							
11-12 P.M.							

	Monday	Tuesday	Wednesday	Thursday	Friday	Saturday	Sunday
12-1 A.M.							
1-2 A.M.							
2-3 A.M.							
3-4 A.M.							
4-5 A.M.							
5-6 A.M.							
6-7 A.M.							
7-8 A.M.							
8-9 A.M.							
9-10 A.M.							
10-11 A.M.							
11-12 A.M.							
12-1 P.M.							
1-2 P.M.							
2-3 P.M.							
3-4 P.M.							
4-5 P.M.							
5-6 P.M.							
6-7 P.M.							
7-8 P.M.							
8-9 P.M.							
9-10 P.M.							
10-11 P.M.							
11-12 P.M.							

MAKE ROOM FOR CUDDLE TIME

	Monday	Tuesday	Wednesday	Thursday	Friday	Saturday	Sunday
12-1 A.M.							
1-2 A.M.							
2-3 A.M.							
3-4 A.M.							
4-5 A.M.							
5-6 A.M.							
6-7 A.M.							
7-8 A.M.							
8-9 A.M.							
9-10 A.M.							
10-11 A.M.							
11-12 A.M.							
12-1 P.M.							
1-2 P.M.							
2-3 P.M.							
3-4 P.M.							
4-5 P.M.							
5-6 P.M.							
6-7 P.M.							
7-8 P.M.							
8-9 P.M.							
9-10 P.M.							
10-11 P.M.							
11-12 P.M.							

Parents should always attempt to reserve at least two hours a day to provide themselves with relaxation time. In my relaxation time, I like to read and watch television shows like "A&E Biography," "Discovery," and "20/20". My husband isn't necessarily going to watch these shows when I would like to, but he may want to watch a football game, and if I want to watch it with him, that's fine. If not, I find something else to do with my time. A person has to really make the adjustments, according to their individual needs and lifestyle. The person who's used to being driven around all the time doesn't necessarily know what it's like to go through the stress of finding a place to park. A trip to the mall might be a nightmare, whereas people who've driven since they were sixteen or seventeen can't wait to get to the mall for that special weekend sale! There are people who are privileged and they aren't seen as having the same challenges as everyone else, but in a different way they have to adjust, too. I was watching a television show where the dad—a business owner—was on vacation and saying how nice it was not to have anything to do but relax. For me, it's the same way. As a wife, a mother and a CEO, I always have something to do; therefore, relaxation time is cherished.

No one can look at your chart and speak to what you should be able to handle or what's comfortable for you besides *you*. Sometimes it's just about planning and thinking about work. When I started my company, I probably worked fifty to sixty hours a week. But I should remind you again that there is no such thing as *always* when you own a business and care for a family. So don't be discouraged or feel like you've done something "wrong" if one day's chart looks much different from the next day. *Do* feel like you've done something wrong, however, if you find that there are no blank spaces on your chart. Be sure to include the average amount of hours you find yourself sleeping, because this may change from what you're accustomed to getting when you first become your own boss. You'll go to bed thinking about ideas and projects you can't wait to get started on the next day, and you'll find yourself waking up early sometimes. Or you may be working so hard that your days last longer and your home obligations keep you up late.

For beginning entrepreneurs I recommend giving no less than the eight-hours-per-day that most of us are familiar with to your business, whether it's in the form of planning, education and research, marketing and promotion, or developing clients. If it's a home-based business, the thing to remember is that you can't become so distracted that you don't pay attention to the activities and issues going on in the house. Make sure you're not prioritizing the needs of your business above the needs of your family, continuously. There are going to be times when you have projects and the business will take precedence, but you don't ever want to allow the proposal you're getting out or the project you're trying to complete to create a problem where the children don't have adequate care or hear anything negative is happening with the family. These are signals that it's time to stop working and pay full attention to the home team.

You may need to make a decision about whether you're going to hire some help around the house or do something additional. You don't want anything to slip by because you're taking on more than you can handle. You may decide you don't want to take on more than a certain number of jobs per week, or a fill more than a certain number of orders per month, or complete any more than a certain number of projects per year. I decided pretty early on that I would only take on a couple of projects per year that I would individually complete. It's important to know that when you spread yourself too thin your level of effectiveness is reduced in everything else you try to do, and you don't ever want to be an ineffective husband, wife, or parent. Where it pertains to your business, you're dealing with your good name and reputation. You don't want to get so much work that, without adequate assistance, you perform it in a way that is less than high quality. It's much better to do those things that you can handle in a way that reflects professional excellence than to get into the greed syndrome and allow yourself to focus on getting more work than you can handle if you perform it in a way that is less than your best.

As your business does increasingly well, you'll need to be careful. The greed syndrome can affect you before you know it. It's a condition that develops when we get more caught up in *earning* than *learning*. It's when we no longer focus on improving our performance and our service to clients, and we no longer focus on finding effective ways to meet the emotional needs of our families. Instead, we find ourselves caught up in professional goals we never had to think about—maybe never even had access to—when we were on someone else's company payroll. We develop a system of checks and balances between home and work that we structure our lives around, and then assume it will remain OK. It worked six months ago, so why should it be any different now?

If you had the same number of children when you started your business and they went to the same school and got picked up at the same time they get picked up now, why should there be any need for you to examine a proven formula? It should be just fine for you to focus on increasing your list of clients, adding to your company's revenue, and building up your savings account to the point that you can buy a new house or new car, shouldn't it? Thinking this way is a recipe for trouble. The ages and stages of your children's development are what will determine their needs. These can change quickly in a six-month time period as their bodies and minds continue to grow and expand. That's not to say anything about your mate. An average adult's emotional development is not nearly as delicate as a child's; however, it's easier for an adult to identify what leaves him or her dissatisfied. If your priority is running your business, that's where most of your thoughts and energy will be, but while making a living as an entrepreneur you should work in such a way that you'll never think, "I wish I had spent more time with my children," after they've become adults. You should work in such a way that you never regret time that was taken away and opportunities that were missed with your husband or wife.

It's not as if there's anything wrong with having financially centered goals. You should always measure your company's progress, in part, by a money-earning standard. A business that doesn't make a profit in five years is really just a hobby, and it could be an expensive one. One sign of progress will be the point when you're ready to take on a staff. Don't be desperate to hire just because you can, or because it makes you feel important, but recognize that it's time to hire when your expertise and resources no longer lend themselves to your handling everything. The primary reason small companies go out of business is because of inability to meet payroll, so hiring decisions are some of the most important you will make.

A good rule of thumb is to have a cash reserve of one year for business expenses, even before you employ staff. I always say don't be desperate to hire, because the person you're in a hurry to screen and get in for an interview may be the one you make a mistake by recruiting. Take your time. I have actually never fired anyone, because I do careful screening, and the way I've always worked is through a family-type structure of referrals based on work ethics. Check references and call on people you trust. Don't call the buddy who never shows up for work himself to ask him for a recommendation on who you should offer a position.

If the work is coming in, then the thought is you're going to have the revenue to pay people. You have a certain amount of revenue generated for your business. In my case, it is typically based on an hourly rate for labor, overhead, and fixed fee. Overhead is the cost of doing business, including rent, insurance, and staff fringe benefits. Typically, an accountant can help you determine this figure. It involves your general expenses. Fixed fee is your profit. The profit rate for my company typically varies from 10% to 16%. To determine a billing amount, you add your labor plus your overhead and profit. The total of these three amounts is what you charge your client. You have to also examine your business resources when considering the hiring process. If you own a trucking company and you only have one truck, it will cost you not only the salary of a second driver, but also the expense of getting another truck to drive. This is the kind of necessary accounting and resource management that you will have to address in expanding your company.

When it goes so far beyond the basic aspects of administration that you become preoccupied with the business over everything else, there's a defect. It can only be corrected by placing the growth of family and business in the correct, balanced order.

You've probably heard the saying that money is the root of all evil. Do you believe that? Well it's not true. How could it be? Money is what pays our rent and buys our groceries. It allows us to clothe our children and keep warm when the nights get chilly.

Money even gives us options that can help make our lives more enjoyable. Try going on a vacation or making a visit to the carnival without it. You'll probably be forced to use a lot of imagination when friends ask how much fun you had! The price of admission is always more than a pretty smile. Money is a necessity of life. And it always has been.

Whether it was in the form of gold, livestock, or consumable goods, society has recognized *some* material form of tender used for buying what humans want and need for thousands of years. It was required for the advancement of civilized communities and nations. It remains necessary for the growth and prosperity of our world today. The ability to buy and sell a product or service ranks in importance with owning the business. Ownership is only as significant as the value of our service or product. Gaining business and possessions through inheritance, for example, can produce assets we really need. Inheriting a family business that's in tremendous debt, on the other hand, might lead us right back to seeking something of greater value, perhaps by selling the business to someone who is in a better financial position to turn its fortune around. This still takes us back to the necessity of obtaining money.

Anything so central to our existence, so vital that it can barely be ignored as compared to air and water, shouldn't be looked at as sinister. Think about all the churches and charities, community centers, and youth programs that rely on donations to stay in steady operation. To a bright, but poor, high school graduate, scholarship money for attending college is a welcome gift, not a reason to feel insulted. And a mother who works a second job waiting restaurant tables on weekends will always be thankful for a generous tip. I haven't thought of a single negative point about having money yet. *Have you?* Money has never been the root cause of terrible things.

The Word of God that has been so frequently misquoted in that unfortunate way states it is the *love* of money, not the money itself that is the "root of all evil." (1 Timothy 6:10) This means that loving riches—more than peace, justice, kindness, and all of the things that are so often jeopardized when we make wealth our priority—is what causes bad things to happen in the world. From depression and abuse to crimes and war, it would be impossible to count the number of sorrows and devastating events that could be traced back to a passion for financial gain. You see, this kind of desire is only driven to serve itself. It's not the same as a pure desire to earn money that supplies our everyday needs, or to earn money that will go toward helping someone else to pursue a dream. So, it's natural for us to wonder how certain people have gotten to be millionaires and billionaires. Many of them will never be able to spend all the money they have in a lifetime, unless they decide to give it away or waste it deliberately. Whose dreams are they helping to make real, besides their own? Where is their concern about justice and kindness when we see them on television lounging in their mansions or wearing thousands of dollars in jewelry and clothes? Of course, there are those who know how to share their wealth and use the money they make more generously than others. This is not to suggest, however, that the millionaires and billionaires of the world are necessarily evil people. For many of them, the ability to make money is its own reward.

The greatest of business leaders and the smartest investors thrive on maintaining and increasing their financial strength in the same way chess masters thrive on improving their strategies against that next opponent. What they give may never be a reflection of what they earn. Nevertheless, there's something admirable about those who are smart and careful enough to accumulate wealth that not only allows them to live comfortably, but to pass it down among several generations. The most recognizable names in America are those of families who enjoy and continue building on prosperity that was left to them by their parents and grandparents. Being born with a silver spoon in your mouth doesn't exclude you from the responsibility to achieve. In fact, the expectation for privileged individuals to achieve by demonstrating true skill and leadership is much higher in the professional world. Performance in the area of business and finance has a set of standards that, despite appearances, can go beyond simple greed and lust for wealth. Therefore, it's important to make distinctions between those who operate purely out of a love for money and those who continue competing in business after they've earned wealth. There's no shame in building success that can be a lasting foundation for loved ones who will come after us.

Imagine a society that would give all of its children an inheritance from which to build their education and careers. Imagine children who can expect this kind of advantage from the day they are born. It may be more than what's realistic, given the tremendous distance that separates rich and poor in the world we know today, but isn't this a goal worth keeping in mind for your own family? The *love of money* has little to do with pleasing anyone else besides ourselves. It doesn't have any requirement of decency towards others or any requirement of excellence from our professional efforts.

The love of advantages and positive opportunities for people we care about is a different matter. Used properly, money only becomes a tool for creating these advantages and positive opportunities.

While documenting your home and work commitments, just keep in mind that you shouldn't try to occupy every waking minute. If you run yourself down, you won't be any good to your spouse, your family, or your clients. It has long been established that overworking can lead to health-related problems and undue stress, so be sure to leave time for *self*-cuddling. This can mean exercising, getting a massage or manicure, planting a garden, just watching TV in your den—anything that gives you personal relaxation and enjoyment. Self-cuddle time also has to include occasional breaks from the work routine. Your journey as a business owner should be one that you fully appreciate. If you never said it before, you should finally be able to say you look forward to going to work each day. But vacation time is mandatory. It keeps our minds fresh and gives us a healthy space and distance from the professional routine.

Whether it's spent on a beach out of town or just sleeping in late at home everyday, the time off is valuable. A family vacation, for the mom, very often, is not really a vacation, because she's packing and she's typically doing a lot of the same things she might normally do at home. Moms and single parents, dad or mom, have to be creative in scheduling time off, too. One thing I'd love to do that I've heard of is to take a week off from work every three or four months. I have an advisor named Jim, who is the CEO of his company, who feels that it's important to relieve stress to give your mind and body a rest.

Studies have shown it takes you about a week to just wind down and feel like you're on vacation. That's why they recommend you take a vacation for two weeks, because you take that first week of just removing yourself from the work routine. I have a continual pain in my left shoulder that is my stress point, so I know right away, when it becomes tense, that I'm going too hard or pushing myself too much. We took a vacation to Arkansas a while ago and I was gone for five days. Immediately upon return, as we started getting close to Michigan, I felt the tension coming back to my stress point. Jim, the gentleman I mentioned who takes off every three or four months, is absolutely right when he says that your productivity wanes if you don't take vacations, and it can happen without your even knowing it. He has approximately thirty people working for him, and he does engineering projects all over the world. As Jim also says, it's important to listen and take heed to voices of wisdom in your chosen business industry.

I have taken two full weeks off only one time since I've been self-employed, so I'm guilty of not always following the conventional wisdom. Now it's different if you're not working full-time and trying to make a living from your business. If you do floral arrangements or artistic painting and you sell your work on the side, that's more of a pastime and it can provide some of the very relaxation for you that others might need to take vacations in order to achieve. Regardless of the circumstances, you shouldn't feel condemned if you don't have as much time for vacations, the same level of interaction with your family, or the same rate of growth in your company as someone else. As you review your charts, just be mindful to put measures in place that are going to help bring the overall plan together. If you're going to school to get some advanced qualifications or new certification in the field that your company operates, it may take you five years, instead of two years. But just because you incorporate new elements into your routine, it doesn't mean other elements have to fall by the wayside. Be careful whom you listen to and what you let people say to you, because a lot of the time they'll tell you you're doing something wrong.

A grandmother might tell her daughter she should be tucking the children into bed by 7:30 P.M. every night, when they've just had dinner at six o'clock and haven't finished their homework. The grandmother doesn't mean any harm, and this may be good advice, but she can't speak to her daughter's need for structure between home and business needs. Maybe the grandmother had a husband who helped raise this daughter and put her to bed at 7:30 P.M., while the daughter is recently divorced and finding her way through single parenthood and pursuing her vision. You can't ever allow yourself to be sidetracked by letting anyone else set your standards—in business or at home.

Often when you become successful there are people who have been close to you over a number of years, but their ability to handle your success is difficult, so realize that everyone won't be happy for you. They may feel inadequate, even though their purpose is totally different from yours. If you let this sort of thing throw you off track, it can take away from your sense of fulfillment. Nonetheless, you can still do your small part by blocking off time on your worksheet to keep in contact by making occasional telephone calls or visits to keep in contact with family and friends. It's good to show people in the circle that extends outside your home that you are still interested in knowing that they're well so they will, hopefully, send you positive energy in return. But don't be devastated if everyone doesn't return your positive efforts or energy. I have realized that in my life, the greater level of success that I was perceived to have, the lonelier it felt. But don't worry, God will give you the wisdom to deal with your success.

Many people assume a person must change when they achieve financial or educational success. The assumption is that you will become arrogant. I had to make a conscious decision to trust God to show me what He desired me to do on the earth. When you are confident in what the Lord has shown you, the opinions of people can no longer control you! When you are doing what God desires, the arrogance does not exist, because your outlook is focused on what God desires, not what you or anyone else desires. If you try to focus on meeting other people's expectations and giving them what they need to be satisfied with you, then you can't focus on yourself and what God has directed you to do.

There is, of course, an important Christian duty of service to other people, but I'm sure you understand the difference between being charitable and straying from your own purpose and principles. There's also sacrifice involved when you're a parent, which is different than just living for other people because you don't have enough confidence and convictions about your own goals and beliefs. Don't ever become an approval addict, because you'll never run out of people to please. Keep your personal vision—the one you prayed and meditated about, the one you prepared yourself for—as the one you guard in your heart.

Stay the course of your journey, and if you find that, after staying the course, you want to start a different journey, there's nothing wrong with that. Just recognize that you do yourself a disservice any time you don't pursue what you feel most called to achieve. Too many of us are simply too afraid of making the move toward starting a business because it's such unfamiliar territory. To tell you the truth, if God had shown me back when I made the decision to do this some of the challenges and pitfalls I know about now, I may not have done it. If I had not been well- prepared, in addition to having belief in a faithful God, I think I may have been scared, too!

The seven guidelines I've offered worked for my family and me before I ever knew how pleasant the results would be, and the guidelines are still working today. Apply these guidelines to the specific timing and method of your journey in creating a successful business and family. Why settle for *parts* of your life's dream and vision when you can have it all?

"Make Room for Cuddle Time."

Seven Powerful Pointers

1. Stay away from the greed syndrome.

   a. Proverbs 15:27
   b. Proverbs 1:18–19

2. Quality time with children doesn't always require expensive outings. Use quality time to answer the questions from your children.

   a. Joshua 4:6-7

3. Remember the importance of implementing children's cuddle time and family time.

   a. Proverbs 22:6
   b. Titus 2:1-7

4. At least two consecutive weeks of vacation are recommended for business executives, along with quarterly relaxation periods.

   a. Genesis 2:2
   b. Exodus 20:11
   c. Exodus 31:17

5. Avoid becoming an approval addict.

   a. Romans 14:18–19

6. Keep the priority and balance in your family and business life.

   a. Ephesians 5:22–25

7. Remember to never spare the wisdom of the Word of God in your business and family decision-making.

   a. Matthew 4:5
   b. Matthew 5:6

FINAL FORMULA

All of the previous guidelines provide a general formula you may apply to the professional and personal aspects of your life. Used wisely, and with the appropriate training, preparation, and consideration that has been discussed, they will translate to your success at home and in business.

The concepts and ideas shared here have worked for me in my life's journey as a wife, mother, and entrepreneur. You will certainly learn, as you proceed, what things work for you and what things do not. Most importantly, you'll also learn what works best for your family. It's never a bad idea to attend occasional seminars, workshops, or conventions that relate to advancements in your chosen field and also to the development of healthy spiritual, emotional, and physical habits in your home. These will allow you to add further understanding to the guidelines you've begun to practice and to build an even stronger foundation.

Growth is the key! You already know what it's like to be where you are, so start moving forward. Take your time, but don't wait too long. The vision God has given awaits you—with the promised reward of fulfillment!

Bellandra B. Foster, Ph.D., P.E.

LaVergne, TN USA
24 January 2010
170927LV00003B/3/P